Genesis 1:20-23
King James Version

20 And God said, Let the waters bring forth abundantly the moving creature that hath life, and fowl that may fly above the earth in the open firmament of heaven.

21 And God created great whales, and every living creature that moveth, which the waters brought forth abundantly, after their kind, and every winged fowl after his kind: and God saw that it was good.

22 And God blessed them, saying, be fruitful, and multiply, and fill the waters in the seas, and let fowl multiply in the earth.

23 And the evening and the morning were the fifth day.

Laurence and his older brother Eugene holding the big goose that Eugene shot with his dad's 20-gauge shotgun. {Philip Gustafson was hunting and mentoring that day which aided in the shooting of this big goose.) This was approximately sometime around November 1948, during a morning hunt at the home place. {This picture may have been taken by Laurence's sister, Lois.)

Goose Hunters I've Known

Laurence Byrum

A lifelong Sully County resident, Laurence Byrum grew up in Troy Township west of Agar. This story is excerpted from a collection Byrum is publishing, 'Goose Hunters I Have Known,' commemorating the decades his family operated a West Sully goose camp.

2023

Table of Contents

    Dedication
    Preface
1. **Oddest Screwball Day**
2. **Elliot** – *an example of what Goose Hunting was back then*
3. **Lyle** – *it's fitting for he saw most everyone*
4. **Byrum Goose Camp Letter**
5. **A Goose Hunting Legend**
6. **Bob Harry** – *the letter*
7. **Phillip Gustafson** – *a great mentor for kids*
8. **Ken Forman** – *he loved it out here*
9. **Lefty Muehl** – *teacher of how to do things*
10. **Doc Von Wald** – *he knew the outdoors*
11. **Sam & Charlotte** – *taught me much*
12. **Shorty & Brian Timp** – *enthusiasm*
13. **Bob Adams** – *quiet*
14. **Paul & Paul** – *hunting together for life*
15. **Larry Masoner** – *a goose hunter*
16. **Matt Thomas** – *friend forever*
17. **Frank Heidelbauer** – *a treasure*
18. **Cale Neal** – *lover of dogs and kids*
19. **Goosed In** – *Barb's bit*
20. **Comments / Compliments**

Dedication

I have dedicated this book to all the hunter who go out in all kinds of weather conditions from early morning until sundown, and they do it with enthusiasm!!

Preface

Jesus is opening this book, he showed me this morning. He made me laugh, yes, he did. When I was done laughing, I knew he had been talking about me. It was not good, except with him it always is good, no matter whether it hurts or not, because he always tells the truth, and truth can really hurt.

But coming from the one who loves us so much he died for us, it is best to just shut up and listen.

I was reading Luke 18:10 out of the New Living Translation (NLT) of the Bible. What made me laugh was Jesus describing the Pharisee and the dishonest tax collector, both at the temple to pray. Jesus explains that the Pharisee starts out saying, "I thank you God, that I am not a sinner like everyone else."

Are you laughing yet? It gets better, why not read the rest for yourself? It is good.

There has been quite a bit written down about this book before I wrote this, but I had been holding back a day of hunting that was so messed up until after Jesus made me laugh. I wrote about that day to try and make you laugh before we get down to my stories about some goose hunters I have known. I have known more, but here are a few of them. I hope you like it all.   Laurence 6/9/20.

1 Oddest Screwball Day

It was the funniest, oddest, screwball day, and I am not picking on game wardens, they can't help that it is their lot sometimes to be amongst us.

It all started innocently enough; I suppose. We had decoys out at the old farm pits that were full of neighbors, friends, and relatives to start with, and later high school students, all there to hunt Canada geese.

I am innocent of everything, I want you to know, as always, clean as a whistle, just watching.

Well, they shot a goose down at the pit, and there appeared to be a lot of joy down there with a lot of running around. Were they fighting or congratulating each other is what I would have thought if I had any savvy at all, but I was oblivious, just waiting for them to gesture to come and get them.

Later I discovered that a banded goose had been shot. Only a small number of waterfowl are banded, and an even smaller number of those birds are harvested. Thus, shooting a banded bird is a rare and special event indeed. There was some mild discussion on just who shot it, but the fellow that ran out and retrieved it seemed to have the rights to it contested. The peacemaker had stepped in and said the only fair way to award the bird was to draw straws or flip a coin, and one of the two procedures was followed, leaving the nice goose with the retriever hunter and the losing hunter expressing to me that he was not happy with outcome.

The geese never let up flying that day after the hunters picked up the decoys and went to the house. The weather that day got more miserable, but just right for goose hunters, especially the young gung-ho hunters who were using a wind vane cow licker for a blind out west of the farmstead. Eventually hunger got the best of the young guns, and out came the crock pot to simmer fresh pieces of wonderful, wild Canadas. As the air filled with the aroma of cooking geese, the teenagers' stomachs were churning, and soon the geese were being eaten.

Meanwhile, the rebuffed hunter, lying in a road ditch with geese flying low against the wind has yet to bag a bird.

Later, our friend and neighbor stopped by to report that when the geese go back to the river, they fly right over the bluffs, and invite the party to join him there for the hunt and the great view.

I along with quite a few others, including the guy who had lost the flip, went to the bluff, and the view was so pretty. Meanwhile some of the young hunters, hunting on their own, shot so many geese and pheasants that they drew the attention of the game warden.

It looks bad, but it isn't, with all the different birds counted, even the ones under the seat selected to be mounted, the count comes out just right. But the rest of us got tickets for hunting the bluffs without signing in, which was required that year, but none of us knew that.

The man who lost the draw, but never got a goose that day took the ticket to court and won.

The youth who had enjoyed the crock pot goose later asked my wife Karen for the recipe. The next day, another hunter called it a 'crock pot of poison', so go figure.

What a day.

2 Elliott

an example of what Goose Hunting was back then

The following stories illustrate that there were goose hunters hunting back in the '50s when their chances for success were hit and miss at best, and slim to none at the worst, but they were still out there hunting.

A mile or so from the folks' place we had dug theses pits and we would hunt there occasionally with just the faintest hope of success. The biggest flock we ever saw light by our pits was seven.

We went there late one morning and were surprised to see other hunters dug in with decoys just a few hundred yards away from out pits.

My cousin Elliott suggested we drive down to see who is there, and as we approached, one big, beefy guy stood out in front of the rest of the hunters, binoculars in hand. With his glasses trained several miles in the direction of the river to the southwest, he waved one arm, hollering "GET OUT OF HERE! THE GEESE ARE COMING! GET OUT OF HERE! THE GEESE ARE COMING!"

We could see no geese and I doubt if there were or that they got any there that day. I pulled up to the sentinel and Elliott rolled down his window to calmly tell the man our story. We have permission.

from the farmer, and we have pits dug and have been hunting this field off and on for some time.

In response the fellow says, "The man who owns the field is right over there," pointing at a hunter that is quietly sitting on the edge of his pit just smiling at us.

As we drove away, Elliott recognized the smiling man as indeed someone who through marriage and inheritance owned the land. Our permission was from the man who share-cropped the field.

I do not recall whether we hunted with them there, but I doubt it.

At our home place sometime later, I was all alone with decoys out dreaming of the one chance in thousands of getting a goose, or just seeing one, when I looked up to find my old hunting partner Elliott driving down to join me!

I went from solitary to getting to hang out with him again.

I jumped out of my pit and started swinging my arms, waving him off and shouting. "GET OUT OF HERE! THE GEESE ARE COMING! GET OUT OF HERE! THE GEESE ARE COMING!" He arrived at my pit grinning from ear to ear.

A few years later, we hunted geese in a windstorm

with gusts of maybe 40 to 50 miles an hour. Our pits were in a fallow field, and the gusts whipped dust up around the edge of the pits and it swirled in our faces.

We were hunkered down in a good field, with geese using it almost every day. Despite the weather (it was chilly, too), I was fully committed to the hunt.

The gusts increased. We both probably looked like coalminers on a bad day. As another gust hit, Elliott turned to me and said the unthinkable. "We must be crazy to be out here."

I cannot believe he said it; my morale was punctured.

The geese came and lighted upwind from us. We waited. Right at the height of a gust, something got them up. It was thunderclap, a bullet hawk or something, and they were putting on one of their crazy fast flying exhibitions that you must witness to believe. Those big geese can fly fast for a short spurt and these ones were aided by the wind.

They got by us about 60 yards away going 60 miles an hour. I think I slapped one shot at them.

We were very much gung-ho goose hunters. And we got to know others just as bad off.

Ernest "Elliott" Byrum
April 29, 1930 – October 28, 2010

3 Lyle Sutton
it's fitting for he saw most every person

Lyle's family had a ranch that stretched about twenty miles from south to north. It was bordered on the west by the Missouri River, and on the east by smaller places like my parents had. The Sutton spread was run by three brothers who had put together the ranch. James had his layout on the south end, John had a place in the middle, and Raymond had his homestead at the north end.

That river was a refuge for waterfowl, so those cattle men were at times smothered with ducks and geese, whether they wanted it or not.

Lyle was the youngest son of James, and the one seemed to be bitten by the ducks and geese more than the rest. I don't know if Lyle felt fortunate to have grown up just down the road from me, but we were at times isolated and he had little to choose from, so I think he made the best of it. Later in life, Lyle and his wife Deanna and I and my wife Karen were close neighbors.

Lyle and I were both from the very start apt to notice wildlife, particularly ducks and geese. Well, it was a bit more than simply 'notice,' it was more like we hollered "LOOK! LOOK! LOOK!" if we saw even a few ducks on a pond when we were the pests that come in the form of small kids. I still remember.

James saying to Lyle, "Yes there is ducks," in a kind of exasperated voice as he tried to keep on looking at the cows.

Our first hunts together were for sparrows, up in the haymow at night with flashlight and sticks.

Occasionally, one of us would get whacked in the head by a misfiring stick. In later years we did some goose hunting together and, later yet we both had paying hunters and friends that hunted with us, too.

At times we would hunt together as it fell into place, or just help each other out. As an example, before we had our hunting camp established with a cook in probably about 1982, my brother-in-law Kent Hyde came up from Little Rock, AR, bringing some hunting friends.

One of them was a chef. Kent said they had stopped along the way to pick up various items needed for exotic cooking. The chef took over the kitchen at the old farmhouse we were based out of. At the same time, Lyle's hunters and we joined in the goose hunting. The two groups hit it off and were soon on a first name basis with each other and having a big time as they joked and laughed and enjoyed the hunt together. It was only fitting that an invitation went out for them to join us in a meal at the far from plush dining table at the old farmhouse.

he table was loaded of course by the chef. I don't remember what we ate, but it was deluxe stuff we ate that evening as tired, hard-hunting hunters joined together in a very good time of eating and carrying on. It was fun. Such a great group of guys.

When our former pastor Ed Schauer was here a couple years ago, he talked quite a bit about the goose hunting Lyle once provided for him and his 84-year-old dad, Jake.

Ed had been determined to keep his dad hunting as long as possible. He brought him to our place, and they stayed at the old house about a week.

The first day they were here, they observed Lyle going by with a backhoe on his way to dig goose pits. Lyle stopped and explained where he was digging, inviting Ed to "Please bring your dad down and hunt every day you want," and so we did. We had great time hunting with Lyle. And Ed still talks about his dad's great shooting, even though Jake's eyes could only really see birds highlighted straight above against the sky and those are the ones he shot - that is what delighted Ed.

So, you might say Lyle provided the crowning of hunts amongst all the geese there was to hunt in the fall of 1988 around the old house the week that Ed and Jake were there. I am sure Lyle and I hunted together on other hunts the great goose year of 1988.

One day this spring, two-and-a-half- years after Lyle passed away, I asked God for help in writing about

him. And then I read Matthew, the sixth chapter, verse 26: Look at the birds; they do not need to plant or harvest or put food in barns, because your heavenly father feeds them, and you are more valuable to him than they are. As I read that, I remembered that the day before, I had gone out into the living room, and Karen was on the phone with Deanna. Deanna alerted Karen, who told me, "There are a million geese flying over Onida!"

I hurried to the back deck and looked up to see a few going over the house and angling to the northeast, not so many, and then I lowered my 82-year-old eyes, and I started to see why Deanna had sounded the alarm, as line after line of geese was flying in the vicinity of Highway 83, all headed north. This went on for some time as I watched and how long had it been going on I wondered? I looked to the east out my front door, and there were geese flying north there, too, but the main flight seemed to be on the west side of town. My hearing diminished, I asked Karen if she could hear them, and are they snows and blues? She could hear them but didn't know what type. It did not matter; they were geese flying north.

Reading Matthew 6:26 I recalled the timely reminder God's geese were giving to all who noticed, about His care for us, as now we are saturated with the news about the COVID-19 plague that is weeping the world. We are called by God not to worry, but to remember Him.

Using that flight of geese and that Bible verse, I think I know what I need to write about Lyle.

He was a gentle man. A quiet man. He raised a big garden that he shared with many, including Karen and me.

Thank you, dear Father, for all that you have done.

Lyle died of cancer. He had it off and on for more than a few years, but he still was netting catfish, planting his garden, and hunting or helping the hunt until he could not.

At his funeral, Pastor Rolly Kemink talked about Lyle's faith in Jesus Christ and how Lyle, in his quiet way, had said "Yes, that is what I believe." Lyle's actions, his willingness to help, seemed to be so good; they were prompted by that faith lived out.

Lawrence Byrum, Ed Schauer and Lyle Sutton

Ed Schauer's 84-year-old dad, Jake weighing a goose.

4 Byrum Goose Camp Letter 1988

Hello hunters!

Here is the 1988 hunting report - '88 was the greatest goose year yet.

The first week in October about 28 geese were using our fields, by the 17th this had grown to about 3 or 4 thousand, by the 5th of November peaked out to estimates of 15 to 30 thousand. Would have been great to have had a video tape of that to show you, in lieu of that let's use a poor man's video.

Just visualize bunch after bunch after bunch until it is a continual flow of geese creating flocks on the ground in two or three places not over quarter of mile separating them spread out over a short mile. Add a little wind causing the flights to be low and slow sliding from side to side tantalizing the hunters who are decoying geese about 250 yards off main flyway. That sets the scene for the hunt of the afternoon of Friday, November 4th.

On the week of 17 October, we thought we were in gravy when using the set of pits. We, after waiting some, all shot our own geese, but the hunt of the 4th developed so fast that we did not get the decoys out before Cliff Stenzel had gotten the biggest goose of the year (up to the 10lbs). And as that hunt developed Cliff's friends, Carl Shaw, Jim Fairman and our guide for the day Rolly Kemink and helper, Aaron Comer spent next hour decoying geese and pretty much selecting what they wanted, although enough problems to make it an excellent hunt. You know, geese lighting just off to the side of decoys plus a little buck fever, plus all the geese in the near distance, you have ingredients for excitement and fun. Cliff and friends concluded their three-day hunt with their limit of Canada geese, 15 pheasant, 2 ducks and some grouse.

The Blacks, Ken and his son John, Ken's brother, Bob and Bob's son, Terry took part in the hunt of week 17th and by Thursday night they had their limit of Canadas plus 3 white front, 11 pheasants, 10 ducks, 3 grouse, 2 partridges. Our biggest success was Bob, John and Terry getting their first geese, we were very happy and thankful for that.

The numbers of geese were plentiful. A hunt at the end of October included Rolly, his brother Randy, their Uncle Glee and Glee's friends from Iowa, Harold, and Glen. Glee made the remark, "most geese yet" in his fourth year up here. Best of all during their 3-day hunt, geese decoyed right in on top of them.

Add to that friends and neighbors getting their geese and you have near perfection.

We were very pleased to have old friend Ed Schauer and his dad Jake come and stay for a week at the farm. Jake at 84 years old, showed us he can still shoot geese. Right after Thanksgiving, a new friend, Larry Masoner, shot his geese out of an old rock pile. Larry displayed an old freelancer's ability to call and shoot geese with intensity and to take advantage of the geese that were available.

We had other hunts and other hunters (we hunted quite a little in December), but those were some of the highlights.

We had excellent help that year with Rolly, his wife Colette cooking again along with my wife Karen, and our son, Greg, Dave Pastein, Aaron Comer, and Scott Sutton. I don't think we can ask for a more willing and knowledgeable crew.

We were able to come up with enough pheasants, grouse, partridges, and some ducks to make each day of our three-day hunts successful.

If the geese just hold their numbers constant, hunting should be great this fall.

Hope to see you then.

5 A Goose Hunting Legend

I am writing this May 1, 2020, forty years after my search for Bob Harry ended.

I don't suppose I ever would have searched for him if had not heard so much about him from goose hunters, and from farmers that, to my knowledge, never hunted at all.

My Dad got to hunt with him once and talked about it. Bob hunted some of same places Elliott, Lyle, and several of us did later.

That he used live decoys was another thing that perked my interest even more, and the story that he was a great shot. He could shoot a load of geese and pick up his rifle and get a couple more, was all too much for me.

My breakthrough in locating him came from a distant relative of Bob Harry's, Irene Chenoweth. She not only gave me his address, but also a picture of Bob and his family. The picture looks to be of a great fun hunt.

Sully County rancher Jack Alexander told me he had a close relative that hunted with Bob a lot. Jack was able to tell me about Bob's live decoys. They were usually a gander and hen with their last hatch of goslings and when Bob hunted, he put the pair together in one pen and the goslings in another and, separated by a knoll or an incline, they called back and forth to each other and helped decoy the wild ones in.

By the time I connected with him, Bob was living in an old folk's home in Harlowton, MT. I wrote to him and one of the folks working there would read my letter to him and transcribe his answers to my questions.

I got more than one letter from him, but only have one of them. It is enough so anyone reading it can tell Bob, though 90-years-old, was still a spirited man. Kind of like the picture shows some happy folks, the letter shows a spirited man.

About that hunt my dad had with Bob, it began like this. It occurred in about the middle of the ten years my folks lived on the north half of Section 6, Pearl Township, a couple of years before using live decoys was banned. It was late afternoon, and they were just returning from Onida, a 23-mile distance for them to drive.

For a person coming into that land from the east, it is easy to stop on the hill overlooking about quarter of it. A natural for a hunter to be to look at geese feeding on the farm ground on the far side and that is where Dad and Mum found Bob and his friend Cole. My dad told my mom, "It's Bob Harry, and Edith; must be geese around here some place."

From here on reader, except for knowing that when they hunted, they got three geese, I am winging this hunt.

They stopped and Bob came over, talking to my dad through the rolled down window.

"Hi, Oliver. Great weather, isn't it?"

"Yes, sure is. Makes it easy on the livestock for sure. Where are the geese?"

Laughing, Bob said, "My reputation got ahead of me huh?"

He was all smiles after that, and he pointed at the field of wheat stubble above the homestead.

"Up there. We saw about 30 big old honkers go in there about half hour ago. As content as they act there must be something to eat there."

"I turned my cows in there because there was not enough wheat to harvest. And I just got done sowing some rye in there. That is why it looks kind of dirty."

"Well, it sure drew those geese in. They came in from the west off the river, spotted your field, swung around it a couple times, and went right in. And there they set."

It was a small field, less than 50 acres, and Bob had already plotted out his plan to hunt them.

"I and Ford Cole would like to hunt there in the morning."

"Yes, sure go ahead."

"You want to come along Oliver?" "What time in the morning?"

"We want to be all set to go before sunup."

"Yes." my dad said. He wanted to hunt with them, and he liked what little he had hunted geese. He found it very exciting, and now had a chance to hunt with these guys!

It was good Dad was just a young man of 32 because there had to be a lot of work to get done to be ready to goose hunt and all that work preparing for the hunt.

They no doubt headed to the house where Mum took Lois, Mable, and Mildred in as Dad brought in whatever they had acquired from town, plus probably empty cream cans. Then he had to get out and do the milking and the other chores. Perhaps Lois at 5 years old gathered the eggs as she was the oldest.

Bob had already taken charge of the hunt and told dad that he and Ford were going to dig their pits as soon as the geese went back to the river.

With shovel in hand, dad hurried up to where the two hunters were already hard at it. Bob pointed to a badger hole, "Oliver, dig right there. It will be easy digging, and just where I want you." Dad dug so fast and hard they said it looked like he was headed to China!

Soon Bob announced, "Ford and are I headed home; we will be back an hour before sunup to put the decoys out. See you then Oliver." They jumped into their outfit and headed out.

After supper, dad carefully readied his Remington pump 20 gauge and reached under the bed for the box of Montgomery Ward shotgun shells, maybe not the best goose loads, but they will kill if the geese are close, and the shot is straight. His excitement growing, Mum suggested, "You have a long day tomorrow, go to bed now."

"Alright I will."

He bounces back up about 3:00 a.m. and makes some oatmeal to eat. He checks the gun over again; everything is working fine. Not long after 4:00 a.m., he starts doing the chores, milks and separates, takes care of everything.

Then, instead of sitting around the house, he puts shells in his pocket and shotgun over his shoulder and shovel in hand, he goes up to the pits and digs his pit even deeper. He does not want any smart gander to see him. It is about an hour before sunup and Bob and Ford drive in and unload the crated decoys, set up the pens and divide the geese. Then as Ford drove the rig away, Bob checked the pits, loaded his shotgun, and along with the returned Ford, they were soon all settled into their pits.

Just as hoped, a frost covers the dirt and blends it in to the landscape. The pits are distanced so communication is easy and plain - another Bob idea.

"Oliver, we were up around the Laurel post office where Charley Johnsons used to live, and whoever farms that now has planted a lot of corn, and it is electric fenced off, and steers are grazing big time. I'll bet the ducks will be there the first wintery day. Ford and I are going up there then."

Soon the sun is changing things; shadows turn into horses, cows, haystacks, barn and brush on the side of the hill, and they see a great wonderful sunrise.

Ford said, "This is one of the reasons I do this!" in an almost reverent way.

"Yeah, but Ford," Bob says, "you are slightly touched, too."

Then Bob got out of his pit and took a gosling away from the mated pair and over to the gosling pen.
They start calling just as Ford says, "They are coming right out of the west again!"

Bob jumps in his pit, he timed it perfect as the decoys are talking and the wild geese are coming.

Dad begins to shake as he gets even farther down in his pit.

Bob says, "Stay down Oliver, do not shoot until we do."

"Alright," Dad says from the bottom of his pit. The geese can be plainly heard calling, and as they glide right over the top of his pit, he is looking up.

The sun shines on them. At 40 yards high they look so big, and he heard geese talk like he never had before; clucks, peeps, and grunts.

"Let them go," said Bob. "Let them come around again." This in consideration of dad; Bob wants those birds right on top of him, so Dad can get one.

Dad's 20-gauge shotgun would go click and not shoot. I figured it probably did that once and he missed once, the next shot the goose was already shot.

Down to his last shell after two misfires, Dad aimed, and just as he shot, the goose fell to someone's gun, and hit the ground beside him, belly up and dead as a doornail.

It all happened so fast Dad didn't don't know what happened except he never shot one.

"Just three geese?" said Ford.

Bob said, "You old rascal, Ford, you shot them all! And all I did was blow holes in the air!"

Now, from the time the folks found Bob and Ford looking at the geese in their fields, this has been my guess at how the hunt with the famous Bob Harry could have gone.

Dad always just said that with Bob along, "we should have gotten more than three geese."

Well, I ended up hunting a lot more geese than dad ever did and have seen lots of great shooters come up empty handed occasionally like Bob did that morning.

I was not even born when the hunt took place. I made details of the hunt based on the experiences I have had.

I can imagine Bob told Dad as Ford went to the truck, "Oliver, I shot at the wrong goose each time I went to shoot, Ford killed it, and I got some wheat stubble on my gun, and it jammed."

"Did you ever shoot a gun load of geese with a shotgun and then pick up your rifle and shoot two more?" Dad asked Bob that because it was part of the Bob Harry legend.

And Bob replying, "Yes, I did. My dad and brothers and I were along a fence row where we knew whites had been flying, and they came over me, and dad said it just rained geese! A shotgun load of them and then I picked up my rifle and killed two more and had three witnesses."

And as Ford pulled up, he suggested, "Oliver, let's see if Bob can shoot a nickel out of the air with his rifle," which he did; quite a fete, but by Dad's logic it only makes thing worse.

Dad had had a long, tiring day. Pitched a load of hay, brought it into the stack yard and pitched it off, adding to the winter supply.

We can figure he slept well that night and Mum had a goose to cook. As I recall, whenever Dad talked about that hunt; it was only three geese and with Bob Harry there!

Dad passed away in 1975 and Bob Harry in the 1980's, so I lost my chance to ask Dad specific details about the hunt with Bob beyond the three geese episode, but I am glad they hunted together, if only once.

6 Bob Harry
the letter

Letter written Summer of '82.

He hunted in Sully County in early 1900 until 1940s.

I had live decoys.

I started hunting when I was 9 or 10. I killed my first goose when I was 10. I still remember the pond I shot him in. I knew every pond in that creek.

Called snows "white-brants" there would be a whole quarter section of them, but they were no good eating. No damn good at all."

I used to kill way over my limit of everything, but I never let anything spoil. I'd give to someone who'd be sure to eat it.

I Lived in Sully County 50 years. I was one of the best shots in the county. Us boys and dad all were. Gift of God, I guess.

Well, I hunted everything there was to hunt, and there wasn't much limit.

You could see right thru their bills when they had their mouths shut.

I still remember that first one. I saw him light on

the pond. He was a big son-of-a-gun.

It was in the creek on Dad Harry's old ranch. (I was a trick shooter too. I used to throw up pennies and nickels and hit them with a rifle. I threw up a nickel one day and you'd have thought I'd blew it right out of the county. By golly, it dropped right down beside me.)

My brother Billy and I went out to bring in the cattle as there was a blizzard coming and that's why all the geese were there. I told Billy, I'm going to get my rifle (a 303 three shot savage rifle) and see if I can't sneak up behind them and get me one.

My brother said, "You can't get one."

I said, "Hell I can't, if I can get a shot off."

I got my rifle and snuck out by the last haystack. There was a big ole' one sitting off by himself. I took a shot- and hit him right in the butt of the wing and killed him! I kept a whammin' it in the flock and dam if I didn't kill 2 more!

Had a plane and we could fly his plane over the country and find where the geese were lighting. This one day he lit on the highway and ran right into Ford Cole and me and killed him right dead. Not too sure he didn't get geese from his plane.

Ford and I were on our way to his place when lit and ran into us.

Bob Harry and his family and friends - 1925. Bob is the third man from the left (Outlined in black.) He was the premier goose hunter of Sully County in the early 1900's. Clayton Wilcox said, "Bob could shoot a gun load of geese with his shotgun and pick up his rifle and get some more out of the same flock!"

7 Phillip Gustafson
a great mentor for kids

There was one fellow that had full rein over Oliver and Edith's farm, and no doubt his aunt Eunice and uncle Elezer too, their nephew, Phillip.

Phillip Gustafson was the oldest grandson of Charles and Mabel Byrum, early settlers of Sully County and Oliver and Elezer's folks.

Phillip was wounded in Europe, maybe in the Battle of the Bulge. He was in the army and was there in our push across France to Germany. He helped a buddy that was hurt to an aid station and was turning to leave when a medic stopped him, he had blood running out from under his helmet, a piece of shrapnel had taken a chunk out of the back of his head, skull and all! He was taken to England and hospitalized and ended up with some sort of plate in the back of his head.

He was always a popular nephew and cousin, now a war hero to me. He liked to hunt and after the war he stayed at the farm and helped his uncle and did some hunting at the same time.

One of his quests was for a goose too. Now the only one besides Oliver getting an occasional goose was Oliver Eugene, Oliver's oldest son. Over the years he capitalized on his few chances and got geese. He and his brother were the ones hunting with Phillip the morning the big goose was shot.

That hunt is well documented by a picture and his little brother writing about it. The excitement for that kid may have been more than any of the others.

Phillip may never have gotten many geese, but he loved to hunt.

One morning Phillip, Eugene and I went out into the field. We spent quite a bit of time visiting out there and Phillip told us stories about his service in WWII.

After the war and Phillip got home, he spent a lot of time with his aunt and uncle, Edith, and Oliver (mine and Eugene's parents) helping and hunting.

That goose hunt was certainly a memorable one. We had waited in pits (someone had dug by hand maybe us; I don't remember.) I am sure it was a surprise that it worked (to me anyway) it was late morning when this small string of 20 geese came from the east across the road. A strung-out bunch of maybe 20 or so geese. Just low enough to shoot as they flew by. One big goose fell to our delight (at least mine for sure) dead as a door nail. I was shooting a 410, so I was ruled out as the one who shot it. Phillip had ruled himself out too, so by the process of elimination it left Eugene as the shooter.

Later we picked out one number 5 shot from the goose's neck: just what Eugene was shooting!

He was a delightful man, and I am sure he was glad the war was over, and he was back. He was so good to us too and good for us, he very much a hero to us and we listened to him.

On that hunt we talked for some time out there in the field before those geese came. They were flying from the east, late in the morning, strung out headed west toward the river. They probably came from the river earlier that morning to feed and were headed back.

After feeding it seemed they would have gained more altitude, so perhaps (like big geese will do) they had been sitting somewhere for some time with intent to later stop eat in dad's corn field.

Anyway, whatever it was that put them on that flight by us created an event I can still remember and see in mind. I was so happy and excited about it; my brother shot the big goose. Boy oh Boy!

THANK GOD FOR SUCH MEMORIES AND HIS CREATIONS. YOU CAN ONLY IMAGINE WHAT A HUNT LIKE THAT MENT TO US BACK THEN!

PRAISE GOD FOR IT ALL!

Phillip Gustafson

Phillip served in the army during WWII.

8 Ken Forman
he loved it out here

I don't remember just how Ken got connected to us, after all he lived way over there in New Jersey.

I'll find out because I have written up almost all of our years of hunting. I'll take a guess now; it could have been through Pheasants Forever. That would fit because believe it or not New Jersey once had some good pheasant hunting. Enough to get hunters there enthused and disappointed when the pheasants disappeared. It left them hunters longing for the old days and South Dakota was the answer for their desire to shoot pheasants, to be fulfilled again.

Now Ken was a goose hunter too. They had, and probably still do, have geese. Big geese, over there and the first year Ken hunted with me he informed me we had lots of geese here in South Dakota, but their geese are bigger!

Later he said, as pheasants flushed, "that one flock was more then there was in the whole state of New Jersey."

When Ken first came (in 1993) he brought a friend, Bob Willis, then later, his brother-in-law. They were having some good hunts and all the time he was mentioning his uncle as in; he was going to bring my uncle and finally he did. Jeff Eldridge was not only his uncle, but as the story developed, we learned Jeff not only steered Ken to hunting, but in doing so he steered him away from youthful indiscretions and messing up his life. Thus consequently, Ken was very close to h i s Uncle Jeff. Jeff had served in the Marine Corp in his younger days, and I am sure that helped him be the kind of man that helped his nephew. Jeff was an all-around hunter. He had an old Browning automatic he called, Old Betsy.

They had many good hunts here with us, pheasants, ducks, geese and more. One afternoon, we had a pile of pheasant, as my dog Jasmine (before she became Greg's dog) stacked rooster after rooster near me. Jeff and I enjoyed the fruits of Ken and Greg pushing of many pheasants down a weedy fencerow to us, as we sat and shot away.

Then there was the morning we went to the little pond on the Evans place (quite well-known for pheasant also) Greg used it successfully for decoying ducks and come dawn, one early morning all 4 of us sat with decoys out in this small pond full of water (but it was not as full as it usually got.) There was some duck shooting early that morning, as the ducks came in and the fun began. As the number of incoming ducks dwindled, a storm was developing. First it rained than it began to hail. By the time the hail hit the down pour of rain had driven us into our outfits and we were driving out in a rain hailstorm just imagine if I was over in New Jersey, out in the boonies hunting and something like that hit I would have been as uneasy as Jeff was about the whole thing. He did not know how big a deal it was or how long it would last We expected the hail to leave quickly, and it did, but the rain poured on. Sometime after that maybe day after all that we drove back down the Evans Road seeing the changes the rain had made the low places in our millet field were now nice duck potholes. We had been seeing geese moving in flying low around this area and all sudden Greg and Ken driving in front of Jeff and I sounded the goose alarm the pond we had hunted was expanded to about 20 acres or more, a waterfowl paradise! Greg, Ken, and I hollered those are SNOW GEESE out there!

Jeff got out with old Betsy fooled around a little bit then said, 'them are not snow geese they are sea gulls." Soon the young men sheepishly admitted Jeff was right! By then great interest had developed in the potholes of water in the millet field. This was ideal because the big round bales were right there to use for blinds and the ducks were already using the potholes. That number of ducks would increase later in the day. Decoys were going to be put out and the excitement gained as Greg and Ken were already out scouting the best spot. Meanwhile Jeff and I stayed on the road in our outfit.

Suddenly Jeff said, 'Where is Old Betsey?' He looked here and there all over the vehicle, it just wasn't there.

Jeff says, "Ken has hid it, I will bet my nephew is playing tricks on me again he does that you know." Sometime passed with no confessing from Ken and Jeff became very worried. We decided to drive all the way back to camp, which was a long way around, because the rain had stopped us from using the road over to the west. So now we were driving across pastures, opening and shutting gates. Jeff and I did that at each gate, and we looked for Old Betsy. We did this all the way to the camp. We checked at camp and finally drove back over to where we started. Jeff was again thinking Ken had hidden it. I got out walked back to where Jeff had got out when the SNOW GEESE alarm had sounded and there lay Old Betsy nice as you please, along the shoulder of the road, right where Jeff, in all his excitement over geese or seagulls had left it.

We had a great time shooting ducks by the bales and as the hunt ended, I followed Jeff, Ken and Greg as we walked out to the pickups and like a tag along kid, I listened to 3 men jabbering and laughing like kids themselves.

Jeff was an experienced duck hunter in his home state which included saltwater hunting along the ocean. He could entertain us about how they did things back there. It was kind of an education of a whole different type of habitat.

Just before Jeff came to our camp to hunt one year, our duck hunts had produced a duck that we couldn't identify, When Jeff got to camp, we showed him the duck and he said it was 'Surf Scoter!' Off Swenson's pond we had got a Surf Scoter, thought to be only seen around salt water and ocean type places. Later Jeff identified another type of duck on Swenson's pond. He was I believe a teacher and kind of an artist making decoys and sculptures.

Both Ken and Jeff had farming roots. Granddad Foreman and Ken's dad farmed, and Jeff worked for them at one time and that's where he met his wife. Ken had gone into the landscape business and did well and especially good in bad winters as he did snow removal. Perhaps Greg will be part of our written memories of those two for Ken and Greg hit it off well. In fact, it was Greg that encouraged me to include Ken in these memories of goose hunters. I know Greg had some good memorable hunts with Ken that should be included here. I know Ken shot a Pintail drake in full plumage while duck hunting with Greg. He told me about it as soon as they came from the hunt and there are pictures of him holding the bird and I would not be surprised if Ken had it mounted.

Before Jeff came along, Ken had hunts with us that were in amongst lots of geese and pheasants and consequently it probably inevitable that Jeff was going to come join us on hunts. It made it kind of neat because Jeff and I are the same age, so, we the older pair and Greg and Ken were the kids on the hunts. Especially around the hunt camp, where Jeff was a good storyteller and a lot of times, they were stories that had Ken joining in as they gave us a picture of waterfowl hunting in New Jersey. Greg was invited to go there and go deep sea fishing, but never made it.

One day Ken was driving a commercial truck and while he was waiting in line to unload it, he had a heart attack and died. We had lost another friend we had made hunting.

This morning (June 11, 2020) I called Jeff. I had not contacted him in sometime and it turned just delightful, like something near perfect, as he was the same graveled voice ex-marine with his humor very much in tack. We talked for long time, and we covered family on both sides, hunting, hunting dogs, the Lord, our health, our family's health, and of course Old Betsy, Jeff said that the call made the day and I agree. I had called with much hope and the hope had been rewarded. To find him alive and well (for us being 82-year-olds different than for younger people) and still have enthusiasm for life. God willing there will be more of those call, I gave him Greg's phone number and Jeff will call Greg and hopefully that will ignite more stories. Ken's death led to one other person he talked about coming here, his young son.

Jeff said that boy is now an engineer and doing great and looks after his mother We talked about dogs he had a Chesapeake now (I believe they are big dogs) and I told him about 25- pound Cuddles, our house dog, and my pheasant dog.

He laughed about Cuddles and asked about Annie G r e g's dog of long ago. And he remembered grandson Josh and his dog, Rainier. It was like a reunion as we talked for a quite a while, I can tell you.

On November 17. 2006 fun broke out. Ken Foreman and Jeff Eldridge came at about noon. Todd, our son-in-law was also there. We visited and then Greg and Josh came. We all went pheasant hunting. It was a blast. You never know when fun is going to breakout.

This is an example of what did happen at some

time for all groups. Jeff and Kenny each got a couple of roosters and plenty of chances to shoot.

Todd had fun too, he stayed and cooked steaks on the grill.

Ken Forman passed away in August 2015. He came here and hunted with us for over a span of 20 years.

George Lovlink and Ken Forman when he first started hunting here. November 9, 2012

Ken Forman and Greg Byrum. Ken is holding a Pintail duck he plans to have mounted.

Josh, Ken, Greg (in ghillie suit) and Uncle Jeff Eldridge. Photo taken in 2003.

Surf Scoter shot in Swinson's Pond in West Sully County, Pearl Township, South Dakota.

Immature Surf Scoter. Female. Medium-sized brownish sea duck with all dark wings. Note large, dark, sloping bill and two white patches on the face. This duck is common in winter on both coasts; often seen around fishing piers and harbors.

9 Lefty Muehl
teacher of how to do things

You never know where you might find a goose hunter, and as a kid, I found one at a baseball tournament.

It was Junior-Junior Legion baseball, and the Agar team I was part of traveled to Frankfort for a two-day tournament. It should be noted that it is basketball, not baseball that Agar is known for. We were the second worst team there if I remember right. But we got to play and stayed overnight to play the next day.

At the invitation of their son, we stayed with the Lawrence 'Lefty' Muehl family. That evening along about bedtime, Lefty himself came in to talk to us. His approach was positive and upbeat, and he was not bashful about sharing his baseball exploits.

He was a pitcher good enough to make it to Triple A baseball in the New York Yankees farm system, but when he got his chance to play for the Yankees, he broke his leg a couple different times. Diagnosed with osteomyelitis, an inflammation that occurs in the bone, and having difficulty walking, Lefty's hopes of playing major league ball were ended.

As Lefty talks, he is getting to know us, who we are, where exactly we live, and when he learned where I lived, he asked, 'Laurence, do you suppose it would be alright with your parents if I brought my old buddy Paulson out to their place and hunted geese?' My parents readily agreed, and that began a relationship that kept on for several years, one that benefited me a lot because I was exposed to sound advice on playing sports and a sound positive attitude.

They came and stayed with us. Billy Wagner and Charley Danks told dad that Lefty and we could use their goose pits. I, ever the pessimist when it came to actually getting a goose, was along and I still recall Lefty was enthusiastic about the whole thing saying, 'Yes, sir, this is just the checker' was his attitude.

Late in the morning, a string of geese come clattering along. When it was obvious, they were going to come over us I heard Lefty say, 'Paulson, I will shoot the goose in the front, you take the one behind,' and they did just that. They also shot a third one which came down over the fence, and Dad retrieved it! I was impressed. And excited.

I do not recall how many times they came to the folks over the years. I vividly remember him taking time with me out in the yard to show me how to throw a drop curve ball. He showed me how to hold the ball, how to deliver it, and then we stood a short distance apart and tossed the baseball back and forth. He told me to just practice the motion and technique over and over, and it will work.

When we went in the house his buddies in typical hunting camp banter started to kid him about being an over the hill old duffer, and for me to look out, to which Lefty replied, "Laurence knows how right now to throw a drop curve, and he will be able to do it." I still remember the impression it made on me then, and I was able to deliver the drop curve, later using the control he taught me to great effect as a pitcher.

Lefty was still coming out in the early 1960s and hunted with us in southwest Potter County. One morning after touring the river bluffs overlooking the bays of Lake Oahe Lefty accurately predicted that "in the future, you will see more and more geese using those bays and there will be more and more geese using this flyway."

Years later as a member of the Onida Indees playing Highmore at Highmore, I encountered Lefty pitching for them. We got one single off him in four innings, and he was an old man then!

A barber by trade, according to the Frankfort centennial history book, 'Lefty is best remembered for his baseball ability, his love of hunting and fishing, and the super short haircuts given while talking about the above.' The Huron Daily Plainsman noted that Lefty is credited with six inventions, 'gadgets designed with the sportsman in mind.'

During his career, Lawrence 'Lefty' Muehl served for thirty years as both a player and manager for various South Dakota amateur baseball teams. He began pitching at age 15 in 1926 and went on to play until age 46 in 1957. He played for a number of teams throughout his career and was often drafted to pitch by other teams during the State Tournament. He also was a scout for the New York Yankees farm system for ten years, and personally knew Yogi Berra. He was inducted into the South Dakota Amateur Baseball Hall of Fame in 1979.

Lawrence "Lefty" Muehl and his wife Lillian Lucille ahoy Muehl.

10 **Doc Von Wald**

he knew the outdoors. And his name meant 'Goose Hunting in Sully County'

The first time I can remember seeing him was when he stopped in at the folks' house. He came in the east door and was visiting with me. I did not understand then why he was there visiting with me. We were neither one of us the best at visiting, but we gave it a whirl. I'm pretty sure now that he knew I was a fellow goose aficionado, a person enchanted with geese, wild geese, but I had hardly spread my wings in that area at all.

I knew something of him. I had watched him from afar, and had been told, 'that is Doc you're seeing out there hunting geese,' but had never met him or seen him up close. If I would have imagined an old goose hunter, to draw a picture of one, he would have looked like Doc. Weathered face and hooked nose, he wore a used brown hunting jacket, an old brown hat with earflaps of some sort, and was not a big man, but kind of wiry. I never saw a picture of him as a young man; I just knew him when he was older, and he was all hunter, had it written all over him.

From an adjacent field, I saw him shoot two geese out of a flock of geese decoying into him. Doc had stayed on purpose after others had left, and as the geese settled in from on high, before they got down real low, still up maybe 20 yards high, those two geese rolled out dead, as slick as you please. It would not be the last time we saw that, but it was the first time I saw it.

He lived alone in a little house. He was a widower, and he had lots of family, but he lived there alone. He fished, too, and in later years kept minnows in a water tank by that house whereas a kid, my son Greg would stop and get them.

Our move to the Brehe place brought Karen and me into his neighborhood. And through goose hunting, we got better and better acquainted, until I have so many Doc stories that if I were to tell them all, someone would get bored.

One spring after I had small grain and corn in, I was moldboard plowing some ground going to summer fallow, and along in the middle of that, I looked up, and here came Doc driving their old Oliver tractor with their plow hooked behind. He never said anything just dropped plow in the ground and followed me around and around for several hours, then took the plow out of the ground and headed back home. Plowing is a slow and tedious job, and what Doc did was just enough help so I was able to get the field done, I had a nice piece of fallow for next year's spring wheat.

He was a good neighbor, and he had connections with the old timers that a young man like me did not. Once, when I was windrowing flax with our old 16-foot Massy Harris windrower, I had it working well; you must, to windrow flax. Good sickle, good ledger plates, good canvas, and good everything and all tightened up and every belt, but one was alright, and that one broke. I was stopped in my tracks at that point. That flax crop, the last grain of the summer, was important to Karen and me, and it was good flax, and here I was stopped. It was evening and I had to find a belt and get it going as soon as I could.

For some reason I went and got Doc, and we headed for Gettysburg and Nagel Implement. They were closed. I suppose they had already put in another long day and were home, but of course Doc knew where they lived, and we went there. I knocked on the Nagel's door, and Mrs. Nagel answered, and as soon as I explained my problem, she let me have it! 'Alfred is in bed,' she said. 'He had a long day. Come back in the morning when we are open.' She had no sympathy for me, my flax, or the 80-mile round trip up there and back. She was very firm and about to shut the door in my face, but Alfred was not yet asleep and somehow heard Doc was out there, hollering from the bedroom, 'Is Doc out there?' Of course, after we got the belt, we had to stop at the Legion Club, and we were late getting home. But I had the belt on and the windrower going soon as I could the next day.

Doc had tame geese that would fly around his place. I admired them so much that one winter Doc and I journeyed into Potter County where he knew someone that sold me some tame geese. It never worked out at the Brehe place for those geese like it did for Doc on his place.

Now I don't want to paint a picture that I was Doc's closest buddy, because I was not. Doc had a lot of people, hunters especially, who looked him up. That little house could really be jumping sometimes as goose hunters gathered after the hunt and there'd be lots of good times at Doc's. He had a piano. It was one of those big ones; it was parked against the wall. I don't remember people playing it when all the goose hunters were around, but I suppose D.J. Martin did because he could play by ear, and on at least one occasion when Doc and I were alone up there, so did we.

We'd been to Bob's where on winter afternoons we would sit at the counter of the grocery store/post office. Bob used the counter and a few stools to sell beer and peanuts and instead of having a coffee break, we had a beer break. So, fresh from Bob's,

Doc wanted to have some piano music and he could not have picked a worse person to help out with that, but he was so insistent, he had me playing.

'When the bear came over the mountain,' and we would sing along. Doc would get so tickled, and I bet it was a sight for a good laugh. To convince me I was a piano player!

If I had a goose strategy to solve, like maybe I knew where I was going to hunt, but not just how and where to dig a pit, sometimes I would go up to Doc's place and ask him. It was through the Von Wald's' (Doc and his son Merle) that I learned about the value of putting your goose decoys out on white stubble, if you had an option. The same strategy was used years later with white Texas rag decoys putting them out on black ground. More than once, I sat in his house as he described how some geese decoyed to him. He did hunt alone some and he tended to call a goose she or her as he would swing his arm around to show a loner's downward spiral to his decoys and he would say, 'She came from way up high. She had the dekes [decoys] in sight, and she came all the way down to me.'

He broadened my hunting horizons geographically. My cousin Elliott and I pretty well confined our free-lance hunting to the western part of Sully County and in the early '60s did not start our hunts until the geese started to show up along the river feeding along the Sully/Potter County line, but Doc hunted some over in eastern Sully County, in Stone Lake country.

Doc and I were over there somewhere. It was along in the middle of the day and a pretty good jag of mixed geese was feeding. They had been migrating and were hungry, and they were staying out in this field carrying on and making a good racket. There was a fence row on the east side of field, and I and Herman Jost had crawled down that fence line and Doc was our 'lookout' I guess. Later I found out that was the role he had assumed because, for some reason, he was pretty sure Herman, and I were going to shoot too many geese and here it was right out in broad daylight with bunched geese. 'Advertising' is what Doc called it when flocks congregated, and then occasionally get up and swing around and sit back down – where anyone for a few miles around, paying any attention, would surely notice them. Doc was thinking 'game warden.'

Some of the geese did bust out over the fence where Herman and I were laying. We were at least 100 yards apart and we both started shooting, and the geese were coming down. Herman and I were feeling pretty good about it. I thought I heard Doc, and maybe I even saw him waving his coat, although I was not sure why. I never really figured it all out until we were up to Bob's sometime later and Bob said Herman sure does like you. What? Herman had told Bob that Doc was all worried and hollering for us to get out of there and I was tracking down a crippled goose as calm as you please. If I had realized that I probably would have been less calm. I do remember when I got back to our hunting outfit, Doc did seem a little out of sorts, but not bad, and shortly as we drove out, he was just fine. I think he probably had let his imagination get the best of him and he felt like the getaway driver at a bank hold up. To his credit, he held in there and never abandoned us. We might not have even shot more than our total limit; it just looked like it to Doc, because of all the geese that were falling.

Doc eventually moved to Gettysburg where he had family, and Karen and I moved to Onida; things really changed. But every time I drive by and see Doc's house still standing there, I think of him. I remember the good times in that house, those tame geese Doc used to have that flew around the yard.
And Doc's daughter, Beryl, told Karen a few years ago, that the piano still exists.

Lucille Von Wald gave the following picture to us and Shorty Timp framed it and it hung at first in the old camp (I showed it to Bob and Merle) then when we moved over west it was on the wall there too. The picture was taken in front of Merle and Lucille's garage at their home in Agar. Probably 1950?s perhaps earlier do not know.

One day in the early 1950's my dad, Oliver Byrum, and Merle were visiting (probably out in Dad's yard as Merle resupplied Dad's bulk gas tank. (Merle was then a Standard Oil Bulk dealer who lived in Agar, SD.) Dad remarked how hard it was to get a goose or fool them. And Merle said they can be the hardest to fool and the easiest, it just depends. Then he described a foggy day that showed no extra promise for goose hunting and shooting. But they do shoot geese, and when they quit shooting more geese would come in, coming in whether the hunters were up or down. Perhaps this picture depicts that day.

Merle and his dad "Doc" were the best of the goose hunters then. Decoying and shooting very, very, well, out of good hand dug pits in places with best chance to work.

Richie Martin, unidentified, Merle, Mark Von Wald, Doc, and Kid Lomhiem

11 Sam and Charlotte
taught me much

Sam was the son of Onida native Charlotte Lieser. He must have been about 12 or 13 when the family returned to Onida from Seattle, and he showed up around our place. Approximately the same age as our oldest son, Brad, they became friends very quickly.

Brad developed several friendships in his formative years that were based on hunting, and Sam soon was one of them. Of course, they did other things that in later years Sam alluded to, but they also had plenty of hunting stories, some remarkably similar to what my friends and I did.

Being late for class some fall mornings because they had been duck hunting, they were like my friend Dave Malloy and me. When we went out in the dark of morning to hunt, we had every intention of being back in time for first class, and I suppose sometimes we even were. On at least one occasion, however, every time we thought we were going to leave, one more duck would show up and soon it was obvious we were not going to make it to school on time, so we'd decide to hunt until midday at least.

That one last pond to jump with lots of ducks on it is what brought their malfeasance to Brad's mother's attention. She heard about them being late for school because of duck hunting and they were going to be in trouble. She thought, 'Good, teach them a lesson.' Instead, it turned out the principal was a duck hunter himself who wanted the boys to keep him notified about any excess of ducks around, so he let them off with a stern warning.

After graduation Sam joined the Marines, but whenever he was home on leave, he started hunting with me, and so developed a longtime friendship, kind of centered on hunting.

Following his honorable discharge from the Marines, Sam drifted in and out of the oil fields and different jobs, and things were not working out in his personal life. Divorced and adrift and in some trouble, I never knew what or why he ended up down at our place one evening, probably at the end of his rope, looking tough and worn out.

At that time, that night, I got up out of my chair and met him in the middle of the living room, telling him I was offering him a chance to work with me in the Byrum Hunting Camp because of Jesus Christ and the forgiveness I was receiving from him, and that He, Jesus, was to get any credit for anything good that might come of this. Years later, I learned it was Sam who taught me what meets the Lord's approval.

As time went on, Sam became a mobile home salesman working in Missouri, Colorado, and in

Pierre. He remarried, acquired stepchildren, and took a keen interest in being as good a dad as he knew how. Sam, his stepson Brian, and I went on some marvelously good hunts together, once when the fields were full of white front geese. Each day, we would get our white front, one apiece.

We lost contact for some time, but reconnected when Sam was home for a day, and we received an invitation to come over to Charlotte's for coffee.

In the course of our conversation that day, Sam asked, 'You still hunting and using that single-shot ten?'

To the 10-gauge, unbeknownst to me after about twenty years using it, I had developed a flinch in anticipation of the recoil, which was somewhat embarrassing, I found out in front of at least one witness, when, thinking it was loaded, I flinched pulling the trigger on an empty barrel, much to the fellow's amusement. I drifted away from that gun, and from shooting.

'Well,' Sam said, 'I got something that will change that,' and then he gifted me with a brand new, in the box Remington automatic sporting 28-gauge shotgun.

I was shocked at the largeness of the gift he was giving, sure he could not afford it, but not surprised because it was so like Sam to be extravagant in many ways.

As we talked, he told me, 'You start using that gun, and you will find you are having fun shooting and hunting again.' He was so insistent I take the gift, I left with it, thinking to put it under the bed and not use it, so that when Sam came to his senses, he could use it or sell it.

Later, I talked with Charlotte about my reluctance to accept the gun, and she said, 'Laurence, Sam wants you to have that gun. Period.' After about two weeks I got it out, and Sam was absolutely right. Using that gun, I did begin to enjoy shooting again. Somehow, Sam knew that, and knew the 28 was the solution.

He moved back to Pierre in his last years still selling mobile homes, and once in a while I would stop and visit him there. Occasionally, he would see me in some place like Walmart and greeting me with a hug, right there in front of everybody, he would say, 'Laurence! How are you!'

Sam remarried and made his home along the Bad River. He had a new stepson, and again the three of us went hunting and had a good time, perfect in fact. With no other hunters around and plenty of geese, we spread out and shot along a fence, I am using the 28 he gave me.

The three of us went back to camp, and while I mixed up some pancake batter from scratch, the Byrum Hunting Camp stuff, Sam and the young lad went on a short mile or so pheasant walk. They came in from having more fun and we ate. Before they left, I took their picture out in the yard holding two geese they got that day, one a white front.

Seems every time Sam was around, there were white front geese there, too.

Sam died of a massive heart attack Palm Sunday 2001. I was asked by Charlotte to speak and organize his service because Sam did not have a church home. I had not spoken publicly in over 30 years and would not. Our pastor, Rolly Kemink, acquainted with everyone in town, knew Charlotte, and after visiting with her, it was agreed that I would write up what was to be said. Rolly read it as mine and conducted the services at the funeral home in Pierre.

As I struggled to write for Sam's service, I became sure Sam had called on the name of the Lord. I was sure he did it before he had that heart attack, and he was not the one in trouble, it was me!

Here is what I believe happened; Sam had called on the name of the Lord, and as the Apostle Paul explains in Romans 10:13 "For anyone who calls on the name of the Lord will be saved." That was Sam's scripture.

I was like the Laodiceans in Revelation 3:15, tepid. "I know all the things that you do, that you are neither hot nor cold. I wish you were either one or the other! But since you are lukewarm, I will spit you out of my mouth!" That fit me then.

As a believer, I had not done what Sam did, living out his life in love. I was convicted.

That week started with indifference and then conviction, then out the other end, with a new love that was grounded in the knowledge that you do not need to beg God to love you; that love is beyond anything we ever even thought of. It is incomprehensible how much we are loved, but Revelation 3:19-20 explains "I am the one who corrects and disciplines everyone I love. Be diligent and turn from your indifference. Look! Here I stand at the door and knock. If you hear me calling and open the door, I will come in, and we will share a meal as friends." He loved me.

At Sam's service, Rolly read what I had written, and then asked if anyone wanted to say something. A man who identified himself as a friend of Sam's through their connection to horse racing related that at a particularly low time in his life when his house had burned down; Sam had cheered him up and bolstered him financially and encouraged him spiritually.

As he spoke, he confirmed that Sam was actually doing what Jesus talked about in Matthew. What Sam did for others, he did for Jesus. And with Sam, Jesus did what He says He does, went out and found the lost sheep and brought him home. Thank you, Lord Jesus, for your love, and friends like Sam.

Sam and his new stepson. Taken in the fall of 2000 at the west campsite. Sam had a new wife, and this gave him another boy to take hunting.

Sam Buol and his first stepson, Brian. Taken the last part of October 1998, in front of the garage at the old campsite.

12 Shorty and Brian Timp
Enthusiasm

When I was the one in charge of grandkids and I did not know what else to do, I would take them hunting, if I could. I headed west from Onida, and it did not have to be hunting season; it might be fishing season or no season at all.

Doing this so many times, I saw miracles happen for all the little ones; a mother duck taking her ducklings across the road, a fawn standing right there for all to see, a young hunting grandchild gets out, walks 20 feet and grouse are flying all around him; a small boy catching a bullhead, a lot of things like that.

I remember it could get pretty happy. Kids love to laugh; if you had a flat tire or killed rattlesnake or nearly run in the ditch or backing up fast to get under some crows; things like that (no, you would not want your grandkids with me, and that's alright then you can do it) really took the cake.

The first time I saw this work I was a sucker. My dad never roped much of anything in his life. I should have smelled a rat when he got me in the back of the pick-up enticed me to rope a steer that he said needed doctoring.

You see, he was taking care of his grandkids, two robust little boys. The steer pulled me out of the side of the pickup box onto the grass. For some reason, I did not let go of the rope, and as I looked over my shoulder as I slid along, the three of them were having a riot of fun, Dad smiling big and the boys laughing and hollering, jumping up and down.

Agar, South Dakota Grain Elevator-Shorty was the manager, a jokester, a hunter, and a father. He once sold some corn for us, for much more than I thought I would get and that's when a good friendship developed. We hunted together, most the time either for grouse or geese, or both.

He had a child named Brian who would pop in and out of that elevator. He was what you might call 'hyper.'

Shorty brought him hunting when he was still a hyper kid. Shorty and I were relaxed down low in our backhoe pit when Brian called out "Geese! Get Down!"

The only one up was Brian, and he was the one hollering. "Where are they?" we asked, and he pointed about two miles away, going away. That was the pattern of that hunt: perpetual motion goose watcher jack in the box!

At first, I jumped ready to shoot, but not so much later. That was not the last time Shorty had Brian along, and so it went until he was old enough to carry a gun. We hunted grouse West River together; there were so many grouse, and Brian loved that.

Several years and lots of hunts later, Shorty has passed away, and Brian had been married, divorced, and turned into a single father, who planned hunting and fishing vacations. Several goose hunts have passed under the bridge, and I am fading away as Brian is stepping it up a notch. What I noticed is he still has that enthusiasm he had as a pip squeak. He would drive out to Pierre from Sioux Falls with wind, rain, snow, and freezing temperatures, which makes better goose hunting. Subzero temps in fact.

He hauled his boy Cameron and daughter Kate along with him as both were hunting geese at pretty young age.

Over the years I have lost track of all the hunts Brian, and I were part of. Some are easier to remember because of landmarks.

November 16, 2001: The two of us are lying by a fencerow. I am dressed in a ghillie suit like snipers use and Brian is well camouflaged too. I have two buckets to carry stuff along and sit on as well. We had scouted this and knew there were all kind of geese using the big winter wheat field we were hunting. As we walked in before daylight, we could hear geese that had apparently stayed overnight on a nearby pond; there were soon geese all around.

About sunup, I tried and killed a goose stone dead. It fell straight down, and it was still 49 steps to him (crab steps because my jeans kept sliding down and I had to hold them up with one hand under my sniper uniform). I killed a small Canada, distance of about 50 yards with Bismuth 4 shot with the 28gauge Sam Buol gave me.

When Brian Timp walked out of that field with geese right near him (he had been lying beside a fence) I saw them get up and then fly back over again. He had to have experienced a wild goose bonanza of sight and sound.

When Frank Heidelbauer and I laid in the decoys, many geese came out of the fog and flew over us as we looked up a goose flying over us just a couple of yards away.

That is something like what happened to us goose hunters. When the geese came to our decoys, so many, we did not shoot because we did not want to scare the big flock away! As the first ones set down, others were overhead getting ready to lite, and soon it was a sight and sound cacophony. With wings flapping as birds lit close, "oh" so close, right outside our pit. There were maybe hundreds on the ground after they settled down.

An eagle came along, and the geese would get up in a massive bunch, soar around and come back and settle down again.

In the late afternoon we watched them begin to feed and by sundown some of them would be going back to their water refuge and might fly over you as trailed off into the sunset.

And as we got out of our pit, there were lots of, "Wow, did you see that?"

Right after that Brian said, "I would like to shoot a blue goose, I have never shot a blue goose."

We talked a little about them, and I told him what little I knew, which was that mainly mature blues have white heads.

At that point, some geese about 30 yards high came, and the closest goose was a blue goose with a white head. They get to me first.

"Brian, Brian! There's a blue! Get it!"

Brian is not shooting, so I shoot twice, missing cleanly. Brian rises, and WHAM! WACK! the blue folds up and hits the ground with a thud about 60 yards away.

"You did it, Brian! You got your blue goose! Great shot!"

I tell Brian I started shooting to get him shooting, which was true, but I also tried to hit the goose and missed.

I wonder if the Lord has not got his hand in this hunt. The shooting gets the geese all stirred up for a while then an Eagle pushes them around.

After a while, a flock of Canadas not over 20 yards high comes right over us, and we got three more geese.

Back at the goose camp, we ate pancakes with choke cherry syrup until nap time, and then went out again to hunt pheasants.

Back in the goose field in the evening, I sat in the pickup and watched as with geese all around, Brian elected to not shoot them. He got up and walked by the astonished geese which got up and set down again.

We took pictures at his dad's house. It was a great day to be out amongst thousands of snows, blues, and Canadas.

When Brian was a teenager, he went to Sioux Falls, and bought a pickup on time, a source of worry for Shorty, who was sure he knew what would happen.

Well, what happened was Brian worked hard, and Shorty lived long enough to see all that, and they had lots of hunts together.

The work Brian did with his children shows. I want you to read this, Kate. It is about a day of hunting with Brian and his daughter. It will be the last entry, maybe. The geese got to stopping in North Dakota and arriving later and later in South Dakota and so the season was adjusted to start later in South Dakota and run into February.

About that time the state developed a goose hunting deal with a big, irrigated farm thousands of acres north of Pierre. Controlled and managed for the public hunter. Brian used that and the surrounding area as the geese hunting was very good around Pierre.

In February 2014, Karen and I headed out to Spearfish to visit family. It was cold, below zero. I was telling Karen if I was not doing this, Brian would be working on me to hunt geese with him as he is driving up from Sioux Falls right now.
Anybody that hunts geese in this weather deserves a purple ribbon of goose hunting.

As of this writing, April 6, 2020, Brian was hunting last year and this year. He called one day and said Cameron had shot a Quill Lake goose which reminds me of another hunt. Quill Lake. Ask Greg about that. Except for the Kate story this yarn is over. I think what little kids like most is playing with their friends. As I started this today, the song, Jesus loves the children of the world, red and yellow, black, and white they are all precious in his sight was on my lips. And still is.

November 30, 2014: Kate is Brian Timp's daughter. She is still a quiet young girl that goes with her dad fishing and hunting. Her dad and she had shot nice buck deer in Potter County on Friday morning.

Brian said the buck stood in one place in a field not a quarter of mile from the road, and no one seemed to see it but him. It stood there while Brian went and got permission to hunt it, and then he came back and shot it with one well-place shot. It is a big healthy 4-point white tail deer anybody would be proud of.

He called me on his way down from Potter County and then stopped in to join us: Karen and me; our daughter Holly and her husband Todd and daughter Olivia; our grandchildren Josh and Rachel, Sawyer, Nichol, Otto, Stormy, and dogs Gracie, Ace, and Cuddles for an after Thanksgiving gathering.

It was fun playing and laughing as the kids and dogs played and the adults told stories, and all ate some more and laughed.

Sometime during that, Brian and I started talking about going pheasant hunting the next day. It turned out to be a fine hunting day, cold, windy, snowy, and overcast, and the wind would bite right through you (unless one was bundled up really good).

Despite the forecast of high thirties, I had put on my long johns and wore a sweater, and as the day developed was glad of that for the temperature never got out of the 20's and the wind was north at a good clip.

There are geese and ducks out moving along with the wind. We were using the Trailblazer. I had cleaned off a place in the back seat for Kate, Brian rode shotgun and I drove.

We went to many of the places that Cuddles, and I had hunted before, and found many pheasants in some spots, but seeing them and getting them turned out to be two different things.

The road hunted pheasants had good escape plans. I had one good shot but missed. At noon we stopped by Greg's, and Brian delivered his annual present to Greg (although Greg was not there), a calendar with each month depicting artwork of all kinds of birds and animals, perfect for a hunter.

Brian had been noticing the ducks flying during the forenoon as we hunted pheasant and said something about them.

Nathan (the one who got us lunch) is my grandson,

Josh's little brother (by age not by size) a miracle walking, a cancer survivor with apparently no hope, but here he is thank God.

Nathan (one who got to be part of my grandkid adventures) said, "Josh said the ducks were roaring in Bloody Run this morning!"

Yes, he said "roaring" just like an old-timer said they did along the Missouri River in the 1940s before the Oahe Dam.

This fits because this is supposed to be the biggest duck hatch since the count began in the 1950s.

Nathan is having a wonderful deer season too, with a huge, bodied whitetail buck hanging in the yard that he has shot Thanksgiving morning. He also with bow and arrow got a buck mule deer early in bow season.

After lunch we continued to slug it out with the pheasants and continued to see more and more ducks. At first, they were just flying around and not setting down, or if they did, they would be right back up.

Then along in the afternoon, ducks in a field not far away are lighting, feeding, and milling around and setting down again.

Our pheasant hunt (that is seriously challenging our positive thinking) suddenly turns into a duck hunt!

I put the pedal to the metal, and we headed over to a section of corn. Not knowing whose corn, it is, we didn't have permission to hunt. Following duck behavior of feeding into the wind, we find there is a weedy fencerow, and as we drive along the side of it, Brian changes his orange outfit to a good camouflage hunting coat, and I let him out behind the northwest angle that they are feeding in and continued beyond him and turn around to watch.

It is soon obvious he is too far west as the feeding ducks have now taken a straight north direction and Brian adjusts to this instead of quitting, he adjusts, keeps working back until he stops just below the crest of a small knoll with fair cover in the fencerow and waits there.

Suddenly, the ducks are all up and Brian is hurrying around. We drove down to find he had two ducks, both nice mallards. Boy. Just what Brian really wanted, mallard ducks! The pheasant hunt had only been a substitute, for his real desire was ducks! Now he had some.

Over the day I hadn't seen Kate much, but I heard her now and then from the backseat laughing at the pheasants and the hunters in a quiet delightful way. Or saying, "I see this" or "I see that." Then, stuck with me, she quietly struck up conversations by asking questions. This took effort because I am having a bad day hearing, and I at first think about just acting like I understand (this may have caused even more humor because my winging it translations can get pretty ridiculous) but I soon decide I want to know what she is saying because what I do understand is good, so I try her patience and tell her for me to hear, she has to speak carefully and separate her words.

Soon, she said things like: WHEN IS YOUR BIRTHDAY? WHEN IS YOUR WIFES BIRTHDAY? DID YOU HAVE A GOOD THANKSGIVING? DID YOU LIKE SCHOOL?

This leads me to reciprocate and find her birthday is November 1st and she likes school and gets good grades. I tell her it is important to get good grades to get a good job and ask her if she knows what she wants to do.

"I want to work in a shelter" she said in a quiet, little voice from the backseat. My heart melted. Wow.

After Brian got the two ducks, I asked him if he wanted to go back to pheasant, but he stated his preference for the ducks. Now on the opposite side of the field more ducks are down feeding. It looks inevitable that they will soon be very near Brian, but before that happens, they all get up at once and are coming, but instead of breaking toward Brian, they are climbing and turning away (by the way, how does a bunch of ducks, most of whom are just a few months old, fly in such close unison, as to climb and turn and circle about) and I start to say something like, "Come on! Some of you twist this way," and then I hear the little voice saying loud enough for me to hear, "Come on turn like on a rope, turn!"

As she says it, some do just what she asks, some, a few and they are high, and Brian takes them. He is shooting, and then one folds, and Brian is up and after it now, he is on the road coming towards us. We drive to him, and his face is something to behold, he is happy. I think because of the nice drake. It is something alright, but it is much more. It has a band, and this has double delighted Kate's dad! He says, "Look at him!" He is standing on the road with the banded leg prominent on this perfect drake mallard!

This morning as I thought of it, I wondered what the odds were out of that mass of ducks for that banded duck to fly to Brian. Like on a rope.

We have another turn of good fortune on that hunt that prevented us from shooting any after shooting time (you had to be there to know what that was) and besides that it is Kate who says quitting time is 5:06.

On the January 14, 2005, hunt, we each shot a goose as they decoyed right in on us. Afterward we picked up our decoys and went to the Fireside for breakfast.

While there a fellow at the next table began to mean mouth Joe Foss, and Brian responded, taking Joe's side, strangely.

After breakfast, as we drove to Birch Street, Brian asked me, "Who is Joe Foss?" You see he had heard me say something good about Joe Foss in the past.

Brian's character was strong and good.

What a difference a day can make. The day before that hunt had been very disappointing. But we had learned enough, seen enough, that the next morning we selected the place to put out our decoys and how to conceal ourselves without handicapping our shooting. The goose I shot with the 28 gauge was near point blank range. The one Brian shot was right about him. We had our decoys sat so they were in a fly way, and we had at least one decoy that moved with the breeze. It was January, with snow on the ground, and probably cold enough to make us appreciate the warm breakfast of pancakes!

I think the man complaining about Joe Foss had a newspaper in his hand and it reported that Joe had been stopped by the folks at an airport because he had metal on him that set off metal detector. It was Joe's Congressional Medal of Honor. Joe was on his way to a meeting of the Medal of Honor winners, and when it happened Joe showed some temper to the folks at the airport!

Thank you, Father, for all of this.

Brian Timp with his first Blue Goose.
November 16, 2001.

Shorty and Brian Timp after an exciting morning of hunting Sharp-tail.

Brian down at the Birch St home after shooting these two geese over decoys on Doug Marsh's land We got the geese to decoy right inf January 14, 2005.

13 Bob Adams
quiet

The History of the Bob Adams Museum

Bob was born on the family farm just southeast of Hazel, SD. He was the fifth child of a family of eight children, six boys and two girls of William and Katie Weelborg Adams.

Bob attended a rural school and later attended school in Hazel. He graduated as co-Valedictorian of his class. He served four years of army service during WWII, mostly in the Pacific Theater. Three other brothers, Archie, Don, and Jesse, served at the same time. After returning home Bob became the rural mail carrier out of Hazel and delivered a large route for thirty-four years. Bob received many safe-driving awards, including an award for being an "accident free" rural mail carrier for 34 years.

Bob excelled at many hobbies throughout his life, including hunting, trapping, and beekeeping. He hunted a lot of animals in South Dakota and other states in the U.S., including everything from mule deer, turkey, antelope, white tail deer, bobcat, etc. Bob as an excellent trapper and skinner and did a lot of skinning in his basement for area sportsmen.

These are only a few of the things that he accomplished in his lifetime.

Bob coached an outstanding Hazel girls' fast pitch softball team for many years. The Hazel girls' softball team was known as a powerhouse for many, many years. The land for the Hazel softball diamond was donated by Bob's dad, William Adams. With a win/loss record of 320 wins and 118 losses, Bob coached the girls to thirteen league titles and five state titles during his twenty-seven years of coaching (1948-1975.) Bob was inducted into the South Dakota American Softball Association Hall of Fame in 2003.

After retiring in 1983, Bob made thirteen trips to Africa and ten more to the Yukon, British Columbia, and the Northwest Territory. Bob was fortunate to complete the "Grand Slam" of sheep. He had to acquire four types of rams for this award which include the Rocky Mountain, Dall, Stone, and Desert Bighorns. All together he took six rams after he retired. Bob's Grand Slam registration number is #567.

Of these hunts, Bob said the most exciting experience was hunting the stone ram in the Yukon, with Hugo Asp as guide. Bob said of this hunt, "A female grizzly charged us, just as we were leaving the carcass. Hugo grabbed my gun and shot it at three steps away. The bear fell dead at my feet, shot in the ear by Hugo's good hip shot."

Of another ram he said, "The Rocky Mountain

ram was tough hunting in three feet of snow and temperatures of -25 degrees." Bob's Bighorn sheep was taken in South Dakota in 1985.

Bob also had on display in his museum the "Big Five," which includes a lion, an elephant, a Cape Buffalo, a leopard, and a rhinoceros. This term was coined by big-game hunters and refers to the five most difficult animals in Africa to hunt on foot. The animals in the "Big Five" were chosen because of the difficulty of hunting them, not because of their size. Since hunters can no longer hunt the rhinoceros in Africa, the term, has been changed by some to the "Big Four." Bob's rhinoceros was darted because it is now a protected species.

Bob had many of his mounts in his house for several years and started looking for a suitable building to house them. He submitted a bid for the Grover School House which many people were familiar with and was successful in buying it and moving it into Hazel. He put in a fireplace and lots of work to shape the building into the museum you are enjoying here today. It was Bob's wish that the family would keep his collection completely intact and share it with the general public. It is our pleasure to grant Bob's wishes.

Thanks for coming, and we hope you enjoy it.

Bob Adams

"Well, I hope you don't!" It was my oldest sister, Lois, was talking. She had gone with Bob, and I goose hunting and heard Bob and I talking about shooting the one white goose that flew with the plentiful Canadas.

"Why not we wanted to know?" "It is the only one and you want to shoot it!" once we explained it was the only one flying over the river hills, we were hunting but there were probably millions of them in North America than she seemed ok with the idea.

I had met Bob because my brother-in-law, Cale Neal, had become great friends of Jim Adams, Bob's younger brother. Jim and his young boys began to come out and hunt with us, and then Bob came.

What a good thing that was. We did not get a shot at the white goose that morning up on the ridge but shot Canadian geese and probably white front too. Before the day was over, we generally would have hunted and shot ducks, pheasant and perhaps partridge as Bob and I hunted everything we could on the short, but frequent times when he came and camped at the old house that used to be my home as I was growing up. My parents, Oliver and Edith lived there with me and my five siblings from 1938 until 1967 when they retired and moved to Onida.

When Karen and I moved to Onida in 1976 the house became even more of a hunters' gathering point than it had been. If everyone who stayed there would have been as tidy and thoughtful as Bob had been, it would have been better, but with no boss for law and order, cleanliness became a big problem. In other words, no cook, and no house cleaner. But it worked.

Bob hunted antelope then (late 1970's on into the early 80's) and once brought this fresh shot, west river trophy to the camp and when I walked in the house that early evening, he was cooking antelope steaks. One for him and one for me as were the only ones around. The aroma of the antelope meat filled the air much to Bob's delight and he soon put the meat on a well-prepared table, and we set down to eat. There is a real satisfaction out of shooting and eating the wild critters you shot. Bob was very happy with his successful antelope hunt and the steak he was now sharing with me. I kept hidden from Bob the fact that the antelope smell, and meat was not working that good for me. I successfully managed to share his celebration the best I could. It was the idea of the whole event enjoyed together that made it work.

My goose hunting a decade or so before had been a dig your own pit thing and anybody who hunted with us did the same thing. They grab a shovel and start digging and this kind of sorted out the ones who did not want to hunt geese that bad. But that had changed our pits now were pre dug with backhoe or 24-inch auger.

Still, one winter-like afternoon Bob and I got the shovel out shoveled one good shooting pit in the snow-covered cornfield of Larry Wilcox. We hauled the dirt away and put out a few decoys. Then taking turns, we each shot our geese. As the one not shooting sat in the pickup and watched.

My contribution that day was a lone goose that showed for me to shoot and that was all I shot. One shot with an H&R single shot. It was a very satisfying hunt with Bob that afternoon. We both enjoyed watching the other shoot good on the decoying geese.

Bob hunted alone one forenoon across the road from the hunting camp on the Larry Wilcox place. There he had a hunt on small Canadas like he had dreamed of. He had Larry and me wondering what happened as the geese milled around.

Thousands of them, it was a wild display. Dave Pastein was there with us at the time, and he too was concerned when it was all over, we need not have worried about Bob, the old WWII veteran did ok. Thousands of geese had sat down and fed all around him, it was for Bob like a dream come true. We were all so happy for him.

I knew he was hunting big game. But never knew how much until Karen and I, on a late summer tour of eastern South Dakota, made a stop in Hazel to visit him. His brother Jim and his wife Marie were there too, and we got a tour of Bob's collection of mounts of so many birds and animals gathered from all over the world. Bob had moved an old country schoolhouse into his backyard and that is where his collection was available for tours. More than once teachers brought students to see it all as Bob told them all about it. Bob was showing his age that day, but his eyes lit up when he and I talked.

When Jim sent us the obituary of Bob's death, I remembered how he and I had talked about faith, and he told me he believed in the Lord Jesus Christ. I am so glad that Jim had included Bob in the folks he introduced me to as we hunted back in those years. What a good thing to be a friend of that dog trainer, trapper, hunter, doorman and a true gentleman. That dog trainer thing was with Britanie's, He was good at it. He had his ways. One evening we were in the living room. Bob, myself and others, a young pup of a dog was making the rounds playing with whomever.

As I was taking my turn playing with him, I looked over at Bob, he kind of shook his head and said, "Not a good idea to tease and play rough with a young dog." As I remember Bob later told me his basic thing was to teach his hunting dogs what NO meant. Then whatever it was doing if Bob said, "NO" it would stop doing it.

During the off season in the wintertime, I sometimes made trips to see hunters that had previously hunted with us. This was part of the business of lining up fall's hunting season. It was a wonderful thing to be talking with a receptionist and being told the boss (be it a doctor, lawyer, president of a college or just a goose hunter) was so busy did not want to talk to anybody then when it became clear it a was chance to talk about hunting, they would either invite me in or talk to me on the phone. I was in a fun business then. On one of these trips Bob knew I was coming to Watertown and had told me when you get done over there you come on out to Hazel and stay the night with me and next day, we will go to the gun show (which I had never been to) So after a great meal with Jim and Marie, I went to Hazel. Noticed right away for a bachelor pad it was looking nice. I commented on it and asked him how he did It.

"Oh" he said in his quiet way, "I just try not to get it dirty." After a little pause he says, "My sister comes over every so often and cleans house." He has the slightest smile. At the gun show I was surprised to see a man there (from northern Minnesota) that had been on a goose hunt in James Bay where the four of us hunted together and as we talked.

Bob listened for a bit then turned to me and said, "I don't know why you would go up there to hunt geese when you got so many out where you live."

A few years later that man came out and hunted with my son Greg. That probably had something to do with Bob's remark. When Jim called me some time back and we got to reminiscing, I remembered this book and told Jim that it would be good to have Bob in it? And Jim sent me these pictures and the write-up about Bob.

Elliott and I hunted for years and unfortunately never took one picture, but some of the Adams family were on the ball and had taken the pictures and saved them.

I had taken the one of Bob digging away on the goose pit because there were not many would do that.

Bob Adams. Circa 1940 before WWII.

Bob Adams and author Laurence on the steps of the old house. They shot quite a variety of animals, geese, fox, pheasant, sharp-tail grouse and a partridge. Circa 1977.

Bob Adam's big trophy goose, hanging in his museum.

Photo taken at the Bob Adam's Museum.in Hazel, SD.

Photo taken at the Bob Adam's Museum in Hazel, SD.

14 Paul and Paul
hunting together for life

Paul and Paul were how they were known before many hunts had passed by at Byrum Hunt Camp. Paul Gillihan senior probably had a lot to do with that first trip they made out here in 1993 but the enthusiasm of Paul Junior and their desire to hunt together has kept Paul Senior staying in shape to hunt way into his 80's, making us here very happy to have them come back year after year. A transition that took place turning those years as Greg became a regular at the camp taking his vacations from truck driving to be part of it.

That lead to us trying to make things more like it was Greg and I even taking certain people under our wings and that is when Greg developed a special relationship with Paul and Paul that continues to this day (3-29-20). 1 am going to ask Greg to contribute to this write up am looking forward to reading the belly laughs and good times they had as they had some very, very, very, good hunts together. Before do that we will write the start of this epic journey.

On October 23, 1993, Paul Sr, his son Paul Jr, and another son, and his brother Mark, arrived representing Safari Club, Detroit Chapter. Also arriving were Thomas Price, a hunter full of vigor and enthusiasm, and their lifelong friend and guide (Ojibway) Randy Altiman. The Gillihans and Randy and Tom said a lot of kind things about us during this three and half days of constantly hunting and shooting pheasant, grouse, partridge, duck, and geese. Randy even shot some pheasants I was keeping for myself.

In the quotes that year Paul Gillihan Sr. said, "Good hunt, the best, everything was excellent."

And Scooby got a compliment (as the energetic Springer Spaniel probably found and ran-down birds.) So that was the start of fun hunts with those folks.

Now when Greg entirely took over (I retired in 2006, but I know there is some fun stories because I've been around when the mirth broke out.) When Paul and Paul are there, a routine was established, come lunch time at camp (which got to be Greg's home) the Gillihans would have a display of wine, cheeses, apples etc. I go no farther trying to describe it and butcher it.

The Gillihans really knew what they were doing. They put out a bunch of things, which I knew little about, but I do believe it contributed to a great time of laughing at each other and telling stories. So, from that setting I am hopeful that when Greg contributes to this narrative, as his memory comes alive, we will have an insight into all that enthusiasm.

This is what best explains the enthusiasm that

all the hunters described in this book and Paul and Paul show us that again and again. (I hope Greg talks about the goose hunting he put together on Larry's land that provided limit shoots every morning about 2 miles from camp (a minute and half drive back in 1997.)

Which drew this remark from Paul Jr, "The goose hunting was so good nothing more needs to be said."

At that set of pits Greg would get in with the hunters and be the 'pit boss'. One morning after he finished a hunt with a group from Florida, I came to help pick things up and one of the hunters (in good nature way) said my son had given him a quick, off- the-cuff sort of dressing down. Something to do with the fellow's timing on shooting. This is how I interpreted what Greg meant, "Pardon me sir, would not be best to coordinate your firing with rest of the chaps?"

In place of the loud explanation of, "Who in the blank shot!" The hunting there was so good that euphoria and good will was everywhere.

Greg handed the telling about hunts to Paul senior. This morning (6-17-20) Paul and I had a wonderful talk on the phone. We covered so much about what's going on now. It makes talking about hunting nice. When I was real young and green hunter, I noticed some big old

Canada geese setting on a patch of burn. I had seen these geese fly from the lake many miles away and then light on that burn. I mentioned it to the old goose hunter, and he said, "Yeah, they do that."

Fast forward decades later a fire burnt several acres of wheat right at harvest and right across the fence from Byrum Hunt Camp. The fire fighters got it out and the rest of the field got combined all right and none of the fire got over our fence. The burnt ground was covered with wheat. The geese found the field. First the snow geese than later the Canadas. Greg took Paul and Paul and others on a hunt there for the snow geese. He picked a morning of dense fog, and this is a hunt Paul senior remembers to this day. Here is some of what he said this morning. The fog was so dense even though you could hear the geese you could not see them until they were right above you about ten or fifteen feet in the air. Here is how thick the fog was· during the hunt Paul Jr. had to really go to the bathroom, which was the great outdoors. He did not come back for a very, very, long time. How long you ask, who knows, but he was lost in the fog walking around in circles, discombobulated. It was truly an exciting memorable hunt. Lots of fog, lots of excitement, lots of shooting, lots of geese, lots of wonderful snow geese.

Hunt number two that Paul describes to me this morning had me along. so, it may have been in our early years. Paul said we hunters laid behind some rocks looking down at some distance geese lite in a winter wheat field. He believes somebody was driving around down there and the geese got up and flew right over us hunters and as the shooting was going on yours truly hollered stop the shooting hold up, we must count and see how many we have, and Paul said it was about right we had our limit of Canada geese! Paul said we had many good goose hunts, but these are the ones that stick in his mind. When they came in the fall of 2001 again, they brought Randy Altiman with them. They hunted with Greg and Josh and had a great time, finished with a great meal and conversation at Bob's Steak House. Paul Jr. is talking about coming again as a strong friendship had been established. We hope to see Paul and Paul again this fall God willing. It has been so wonderful to hunt with so many fine folks.

    Thank you, dear Father, for it all.

*Paul Sr, his sons (Mark and Paul Jr) and Randy Altiman.
Kneeling in front: Tom Price, October 23, 1993.*

*Greg Byrum, Paul Sr., Paul Jr. and unidentified
This duck hunt was one of the best of all time!
November 12, 2000.*

*Paul Sr, Laurence Byrum and Paul Jr.
They are also pheasant hunters.*

15 Larry Masoner
a goose hunter

Larry and I traded letters for 5 years before this Texas goose hunter came up to our hunt camp. It was November 1988. I have his picture dated November 28, 1988. Larry hunted geese in the Texas panhandle and up in the Tishomingo National Wildlife Refuge area. He also mentioned Hagerman area which is at the Texas, Oklahoma border. There he hunted in winter wheat fields that would have water holes with rocks piled in them, maybe they were dugout to put rocks in. He said the geese would use those water holes on occasion before they went back to the refuge.

Larry would find his hunting spots by using good binoculars and watching the geese go by several miles from the refuge to feed sometimes. He would take coordinates and it might take over a day for him to find the field they were in. Then he would go to work on them.

He worked hard for an oil company and his wife Deanna worked hard too. These hunts must have been coordinated with time off and long weekends. If the geese were using the rock pile dugouts (actual note show, they may have been rock quarries) he had some old mail sacks he used for camouflage that looked like rocks and he would let loners and such lite right in the ponds so flocks would follow right into the decoys. Otherwise, he used whatever would work. If he found a pond that worked, he would leave it alone for weeks before he used it again. He also hunted out west in the panhandle north of Amarillo. The wheat farmers in the panhandle had so many geese at times after they got to know Larry at least one of them offered him the key to his gas tank (as it was long drive back and forth to there) and all the shells if he would just shoot the heck out of the geese and get them off his fields. He would not do that though, he was an aggressive hunter, but he did not slaughter game. These hunts in those areas provided him with snow geese, specs, and Canada's.

We spent part of a day here watching geese on the home place. They fed there and in surrounding area and as we watched we figured out a few of the big geese were sorting themselves away from the thousands of other geese and feeding on sunflowers right around the old rock pile in center of home section 34.

Back in the 70's Ed Schauer had helped me take out a half of mile of divide fence there and we added to an already small rock pile (there was a modest amount of rock on section 34) and Ed declared that would be a place for his dad to come and shoot geese, and it was, which is another story.

On the 27th of November 1988 Larry and I saw our

plan develop. We were going to set up at the rock pile for those few big geese that fed on the sunflower heads that were left (I think by the combines turning away from the rock piles) and only the methodical big geese had located those heads of sunflowers. At that time, in our area, that was unusual, as most of the geese preferred milo, millet, winter wheat and corn.

We lingered, Larry and I in the cook shack the next morning, long after everyone else was out and about. Part of it was because we had the geese, we were hunting pretty-well scouted, and we just wanted to set and talk. We had talked by phone and wrote letters (he had seen our ad somewhere years ago) it was nice to talk face to face. We had a lot of ground to cover during our visit. Two goose hunters relishing that. We left the shack about 9:30 am and the hunt worked just like we had hoped, and we were able to get some of those sunflowers eating big ones. Larry did most of the calling and shot most of the geese!

Sometime after that Karen and I took a plane from Little Rock, where we were visiting Kent and Betty Hyde to Houston to see Ed and Ila Schauer. They were living in Huntsville, Texas then, and the plane made a stop at Love Field in Dallas and Larry picked us up and we were guests at he and Deanna's home.

They took us out for a Tex-Mex meal which I had

showed some curiosity about. It was great! That way Karen and I got to meet Deanna and we got to see the nice layout of their place before we continued to Houston.

Larry Masoner with his three big Canadian Geese.

Karen and I received the following note from Deanna Masoner (8/2022)

The Byrums,

I understand that I'm taking a chance but was going thru some of the things I need to downsize. Of course I remember you both and was blessed enough to know what fine people you are. Larry loved the conversations with Lawrence so much and had so much respect for you both. Remember meeting you both.

I just turned 80 yrs on June (Believe it)

Larry has been gone for over 11 yrs. and still miss him. He does occ. tap me on the side of my head and remind me to pay attention as he always said "pay attention to details". Have to smile and think of him. Like it better now than when I was lying !! Ha.

Hope this finds you both doing ok. I didn't have your number but have your address.

Just to say you both made me smile when I came about your letters to Larry. Your family is very blessed and hope I hear back. Every day is a Gift.

(Hugs + Prayers)
Deanna Masoner Aug 2022

16 Matt Thomas
friend forever

It was probably the third week October in the year 1985 and the geese were flying low all over our fields. It was the first time Matt and his friend J W Walsh had ever been here. These experienced quail hunters were getting a sight they had never seen before as they lay on their backs in the old pit and watched flock after flock of low flying geese right above them.

The following story is about a friendship that developed over 20 plus years of many hunts, many letters and phone calls.

When I first met him, I didn't know much about him. I soon learned he was a single parent raising children and he and his brothers operated hardware stores in Jacksonville Florida. But here was the kicker he lived in the country out west in Duval County. Out on Cemetery Road where he ran a few head of cattle and commuted to work over the St. John River. He had two old neighbor buddies and the 3 of them formed an exclusive hunting club (later they let me be an Honorary, non-voting member and exclusively for me, made a framed signed membership certificate!) They were a close-knit club and continued to talk about my membership jokingly.

I learned his address because we exchanged letters

filled with hunting talk. The hunting club disappeared during those years when a gal they called the "widow Mary" came along and won Matt over. He dropped out of the club and married her but not before the club had hunted up here.

Also, his sons, Gabe and Shane had all at one time or another come here and hunted. Not that he quit hunting when he got married because he kept coming up here until 2008.

I was down there in 2012 and met Mary and had a reunion of hunters out at his place on Cemetery Road. It was right during the spring Turkey season in Florida and Matt's grandson, Hunter, shot his first wild turkey before the day was over. Matt and his friends were some of the hunters, those years of the 1980's on to 1995 staying in the old farmhouse with a trailer house cook shack alongside. We had some good times there but during that time the old Artisan well quit so water hauling became part of the work along with cleaning birds and picking up and taking people to the airport I could meet myself coming and going. But we shot a lot of geese and people were rebooking.

In 1996 we moved three miles west leaving the old house (when we moved Tim Thomas said he liked the old house, and some others liked it too.) The water for the new camp was plentiful and we were in a more secluded place right about where my parents lived before and during the dirty thirties. I loved the place. I wanted plenty of water and privacy and we found that there. It proved to be and still is a natural pheasant habitat. We were blessed with not just one but three ponds to hunt ducks on all within less than a mile from the front door. We could walk to them if we chose to.

During those years Greg got to be more and more a duck decoying and duck calling person and Matt and Tim turned into duck hunters. It was the first hunt of the day in the dark of morning the duck hunters would head out and I would either finish cleaning up the breakfast mess or as we changed to brunch in a few years get the pancakes ready and table set for brunch.

Often, I would be up before sunup and hear the fellows talking. What a relief the ducks were showing up again. One morning the duck hunting was not working, and everybody left but Matt and Tim. They stayed and waited. Along about 11 o clock it started to snow and with the snow the ducks came, and they were rewarded with a good duck shot. Kind of like Doc, waiting alone for the geese to fly.

Something else special developed that helped cement some good friendships. Visiting. Just plain old visiting. In 1996 (later I'll tell you more about

Matt coming to hunt with me then)

Matt brought a wonderful old guy George Young (he was about my age) and Matt's late teen sons, Shane and Gabe. We had a great hunt and so much fun. We found those pheasants. At least one whitefront and Canada geese and ducks. Matt playfully accused me of favoring George, and we all saw Karen favoring the two boys with fresh cooked brownies and things like that. The last evening the boys came in from our spring filled area (another bonus at the new location) with some green winged teal to cap off the three-day hunt. Matt and Tim kept coming back until 2008. The habit of visiting developed. Partly because I turned bird cleaning over to folks in Onida and then had evenings free.

We would begin visiting after supper in our living room of chairs and sofas. Sometimes Matt would break out some potato chips and the bag would be passed around (I got to calling it Camp Luxury, but it was just an old mobile home cleaned up the best we could). What I grew to like more than anything was our early, early, morning talks that started over at our west camp, I would be up first than Matt (these early morning visits later fit some people that hunted there too) would get up before the others. It would be so quiet as we talked. We sat visiting at the far end of the mobile home, the same place as the evening visits. At first it was just Matt and I getting better acquainted. Then others might come and join in. As we got to talking you never knew which topic we would cover, but if it got too political or too serious Matt would say he didn't want to hear about it and steer the conversation back to more productive things.

One morning his friend and longtime hunting partner, JW had captivated us with his stories about his life in the service and other things.

I later said to Matt, "I never knew JW had (JW had been to the Northern Territories, as Matt called South Dakota, a few times) so many far-flung adventures."

Matt said he had heard stories himself, but he had never heard some of those stories before!

Matt's first year here, there were geese all over the place. Charley Caddell had been coming up from Jacksonville for couple years and the year before Matt came, as Charley was leaving, he said, "I'm coming again next year, and I'll bring some guys who can shoot" Matt and JW were them fellas.

That first morning we had a pit full at our big covered permanent shooting affair, so we put Matt and JW in an old hole about 200 yards or more away. They were good boys, never shot to many geese, in fact they used the big old caved in backhoe pit to just look up as hundreds and hundreds of geese flew right over them. They had never seen anything like that before. It was great that they got off to good start because leaner years were coming to Byrum Hunt Camp.

We were, the first years, blessed with thousands and thousands of geese and some pheasants and ducks, then we had some poor years with almost no pheasants and the geese alone were it.

Then came the fall of 1989, the geese did not show early. It looked no different than usual; I had the fields ready and kept out of the way (meaning nothing to bother incoming migrating geese). I expected some real early migrators to start feeding on our place, which they did, but the numbers never increased and they themselves quit coming also. But still I was confident some would show they always had by the third Saturday in October.

That week I would begin our 'out of state' hunts when they could hunt pheasant and most anything else. The hunting had been good enough the proceeding years Matt and JW did not just come themselves; JW brought his son; they brought nephews and friends of their kids and Matt's brother Tim was there with his son. All we were shooting were sharp-tail grouse. It was so warm they killed a rattlesnake too. Thank goodness for the sharp-tails.

Even the ducks were giving us the slip.

About the 2nd day after lunch, before upland game time JW and Matt very neatly sat down with me at the table in the dining room of our cook shack.

JW said, "Laurence, you said the geese would be here. What happened?"

I told them the same thing I have written above and that going by previous years the geese should have been there. It was a very good meeting; a model of what hunters can do when things are not working. They designate a spokesman, talked it over to find out what the hunt provider had to say and how he said it and gave him a chance to explain the situation. (I did take some action that really helped. This is told as a secret in another part of Matt's story.)

Their plane left for Jacksonville on a Sunday morning and a weather front came in behind them, the fields were full of geese that afternoon. I talked to Lyle on the phone late Sunday, and he told me the geese had moved in and we were shooting them on Monday morning (Sam Buol and his stepson Brian) right where nothing was going on 48 hours before.

Matt was still hunting with us for over another 20 years and JW came back various time as did Tim, right along with many new friends, like George

Young, Larry Wroten, Jimmy Jones, Don Ruckman, Lee Smith, Matt's sons Shane and Gabe, brother-in-law Keith (these are just a few names from off the top of my head) and many more. Matt and JW's goodwill produced many more good hunts over 2 more decades.

After the drought years of pheasant my goal was to create habitat good enough right around our camp so a hunter could put his boots on grab his shotgun and go out the door and shoot some pheasant. That became a reality and happened on several different occasions. No one used it more than Matt and Tim.

Greg began living at the camp and he got some food plots planted within 100 yards or so of the front door. One was a small cornfield. I remember Matt and Tim out there on a least one occasion shooting roosters in the middle of the day, in plain sight of the front door of camp.

The birds would slip in and out of there, you just had to watch and catch them when they were in there. This was the hunters that had traveled with me, from our camp, over 200 miles (round trip) for a pheasant shoot and at least one of those trips produced very little. The hunting got so good it seemed each year was topped by the next until we almost got used to walking out the door and getting our limit right close to our camp as the Conservation Reserve Program and great weather produced numbers we had only hoped and prayed for.

To add to the understanding of what our camp was like is what Howard Carlson noted in his quote for our brochure, it was, he said, "The variety of game." Some years (and Howard was there a lot) we shot grouse, prairie chicken, ducks, geese, multiple kinds of geese, ducks and pheasant and some hunters shot crane. Howard and I used his big suburban for a least one fox hunt chase and I can think of other fox chases with other hunters too!

We had a place called the hog lot. Dad had fixed it up with woven wire fence all around it and dug a pond there on about 20 acres and he would move his April pig crop down there for the summer about mile from the house (good idea no smell then by the house). Later we used it for bull pasture and then for our hunting. It was a kind of a game reserve because of the food plot and all. It did attract game. I once stood there as we were hunting pheasant and witnessed this: ducks flushed off the pond, partridges in the air with grouse and pheasants all flying at the same time. Maybe some geese overhead I do not remember, but there were plenty times that scene could have also included geese too. It was fitting that the hog lot would be the place to represent the accumulation of all the years Matt and Tim had been coming and our first glimpse of the biggest hatch yet would all coincide as the Thomas brothers, Don Ruckman, Lee Smith, Greg and I made a planned out move on the food plot, never dreaming (maybe dreaming but still not ready for what happened) of the event we were about to see. Matt and I had come in from the northeast moving toward food plot. Don and Lee were in position to the southeast about hundred yards from the plot in anticipation of pheasants flying out over them, escaping to the CRP right behind them. Greg was coming in from northwest and Tim straight in from the north.

Matt and I had each shot a pheasant on the way in and when that shooting stirred little activity, I think we thought there may be some holding tight perhaps, but probably not a lot, leaving us completely unprepared for what happened. As Tim and I met, I turned south to join him in a walk down the center of food plot with Greg and Matt kind of flanking us on either side with the dogs behaving themselves because no birds were being chased up a head of us. As Tim and I start to move a series of pheasants get up in waves resembling the waves you see at major league baseball games. Each wave is started by Tim shooting a pheasant right in front of him and Greg and I are watching saying wow, man, oh man, oh man at the awesome sight of it all.

Then Tim would shoot another rooster and another wave would start out in front of where Tim was shooting. Tim is standing in one place shooting, as one rooster falls another gets up for Tim and he is not missing. These waves reach from him to the far end of the plot about 150 yards and as this is going on Don, Matt, and Lee are shooting and roosters are dropping from the flights breaking to the east headed for cover out there. Tim continues shooting and Greg and I keep cheering him on. He had stood in that one spot and bagged 5 birds, filling his 3-bird limit and 2 extra to fill my 3-bird limit. We are still in total surprise at the sight. By the end of that shoot everyone had their bird limit, totaling 18 birds, shot at that one small area.

When I think back on that I cannot help but tie that to JW and Matt and that patient talk they had with me years before. We have plenty more good pheasant shoots during those years, just like we had hoped and prayed for.

Greg and I had advertised pheasant hunting at its best as you and friends or family walked with dogs in good cover shooting pheasant. Matt and Tim added 2 new wrinkles. One, where we watched, and they walked. They moved very,

very slowly and occasionally Matt would whistle like (I guess he did quail hunting) to get the birds to react. Then another way, without dogs they would hunt spread out and when they shot a bird and it fell, they would not shoot again until they found that one.

Each brother would mark the bird down exactly and immediately each hunter would begin a walk to their spot and where the trails crossed the bird should be there. This demanded a dead bird not cripples if hunting with no dog. They travel all the way up here as brothers and they like to hunt that way too. No story about Matt and his impact here would be complete if I did not include how he disregarded a bad report on me and my hunting camp and brought his two sons Shane and Gabe and his old friend George Young up here hunting that year of 1996.

I suppose at our early morning visit I brought up that unhappy subject because the man was from Jacksonville, and I told Matt about my worries about him hearing about that low opinion of me and him not coming because of that. Matt said he knew about the whole thing as soon as they got to town and pretty much disregarded it and proceeded to secure a hunt here.

We had a wonderful hunt and Matt booked right

back in and came every year after that for 12 more years. I will not forget that. Matt and Tim's character are revealed in these stories. Good friends of ours. Matt called our locale the 'northern territories' and he came here a lot, bringing friends and family. And yes, I think he added goose hunter to his list of things he was.

A very good friend, he was. Matt had his first heart attack out in the Georgia wood. As he lay alone waiting for help (his hunting partner was getting him help) he was praying, talking to God, as a squirrel up in the tree he was laying under scolded him. He forgave everyone he had anything against and asked for forgiveness of his sins and soon he was in a helicopter headed for the hospital in Jacksonville and a new way of life.

He started to work out, eat right and generally take care of his health. He went for walks with Mary for one thing. And he kept coming up here each fall. Even after he had another one. He called me one day with one of his wonderful fresh hunting adventures. He had been up in Georgia hunting deer, there was an older man sharing the hunt and he heard the fellow shoot and went over there because he thought the old fellow might need help. He did. He had a good-sized buck much to their delight and needed lots of help loading him up.

As Matt talked, he said, "I must have strained myself, it feels almost like a cracked rib." It turns out they found cancer. We stay in contact. Then his brother-in- law calls me says Matt passed away. He tried to cheer me up and told me, "Although he was hospitalized for cancer, he had another heart attack and died with Mary laying by his side. "

"Laurence," he says, "he was going to suffer with that cancer and all of us around him felt like he avoided much more pain."

I sat out on the back deck the afternoon of Matt's funeral and looked up into the clear blue sky and wave after wave of high-flying snow geese were flying northwest right out towards the old place 20 miles away. That night Greg called me and said, "Dad the fields out here where there were no geese are loaded with snow geese now."

It was the spring migration, and it was the first time (or any other time) we had ever had that many snow geese around there. It was estimated at one hundred and fifty thousand in a five-mile radius or less of the old hunting camps that Matt, his friends, and family had stayed in. They were feeding in some of the fields he had hunted and flying over where he had slept and ate and visited with me in the early mornings.

We hunted them some, as grandson Josh and son Greg got quite a few (I shot one,) The geese left in about two days. I called it the Matt Thomas Memorial hunt. And yes, I took that mass of geese there at that time as a sign from heaven.

I have the letters from Matt and the signed certificate from the three members of the THERAPEUTIC HUNT & FISH CLUB signed by Matthew L Thomas, Lawrence S. Wroten, and George Young and lots of memories wrote out in the Hunting Reports each year. But you know what is so good? Each one of those men, now departed, gave every evidence and said so in faith that they believed in the Lord Jesus Christ, so even though the quick death of Matt made me know how much I would miss him, the joy of the hope of everlasting life and us all being in heaven forever beats everything else (all that stuff) by far.

The more I live the more I believe it is all about Jesus and that he shed his blood for our sins and the great love he and our dear Father in heaven has for us. That is why he had to rid us sinners of sin if we ask, so we could be with them forever.

NLT "For God so loved the world that he gave his only Son, so that everyone who believes in him will not perish but have eternal life. Amen," John 3-16.

Matt Thomas and his brother, Tim.

Tim and Matt Thomas.

Laurence, Gabe, Shane and George Young. 1996.

Shane Thomas. Matt's son. 1996.

Shane and Gabe Thomas with a beautiful Mallard Duck.

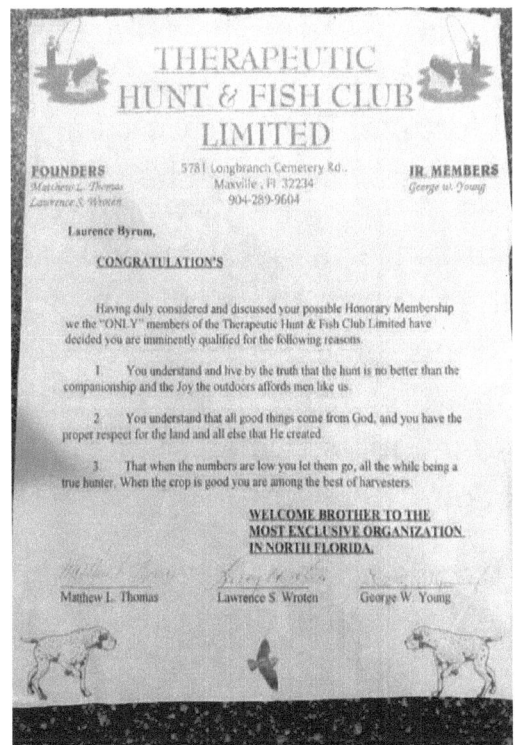

FTHERAPEUTIC HUNT & FISH CLUB
signed by Matthew L Thomas, Lawrence S.
Wroten, and George Young.

17 Frank Heidelbauer
a treasure

Down in Sioux Falls, South Dakota back in the early 1990's there was a Presbyterian Church that, after church each Sunday they served coffee while people sat and visited. On one Sunday my friend, Rolly Kemink, was there visiting his old home church.

Also, on that same Sunday Frank Heidelbauer was there. As Rolly stopped to visit with Frank (who knew Rolly was the minister of the Presbyterian church in Onida) asked Rolly if there was anywhere out around Onida that he may be able to hunt geese. To my good fortune, Rolly gave him my name; what a good thing that turned out to be!

The afternoon of December 8, 1993, I was out by our grain bin attending to the auger as corn was being combined. Frank pulled up and at his beckoning I climbed into the front seat of his outfit. He proceeded to tell me a real good story. That was the beginning of our friendship.

He was an excellent storyteller and he his ability to spellbind me was kind of like Lefty Muehl.

Frank had flown supplies over the hump to General Stillwell in China during World War II. When he got out of the service, he did some crop dusting. It was a dirty job and finally Frank just left the plane and walked off! He did several other good and exciting things, but I am not going to try and tell you them like he did, but he talked for a long time. The two key things that probably connected us were his rapture with ducks and geese.

As a kid in Iowa, he lived on a farm and raised Mallard ducks. He did his best to try to quack like a duck. In his later years he custom made duck and geese calls. They were high priced, but people got in line to have a special Heidelbauer call. Each winter he took time to carefully make them. As he talked, I listened, and I felt I had met another unique and special person that loved goose hunting like I did. It was early afternoon when he came and soon geese began to fly over the place. Frank and I drove where we could watch and what we saw was enough to get a 70+ year old hunter excited and that attitude was special to me.

We had a great hunt for Frank, he was a grand champion goose caller in nationwide contests twice and later he was a judge of the contests.

Over the next two days, early each morning Frank and his son, Jeff would show up in plenty of time so we could put to gather Jeff's big foot decoys and get set to shoot geese (out of a good, backhoed pit I had been using all fall.) They couldn't have come at a better time as there were plenty of geese around.

The geese were using a winter wheat field north of the corn field where we were at, and they were also using a millet field to the west of us. When they left the winter wheat, they flew over the corn field going on east, but sometimes they fly into the corn where we were hunting. So, we not only got to shoot the geese we had them near and far all the time. Some would act like they would decoy and slide on, but some decoyed perfect and we got our six-goose limit. Then we would take some pictures, pick up the decoys. The next day we did the exact same thing.

What a great start to a solid friendship.

I wrote about the December 1995 goose hunts and noted we always looked forward to hunting with Frank and Jeff Heidelbauer. The day before they came in the weather was nice and balmy. I did some work around the place and then helped Otto and Ozzie (they were local goose hunters) shoot some nice geese out in the millet field. At midnight the weather had changed bringing fifty mile an hour winds and snow. The temperature dropped below zero, so we had to cancel our December 8th hunt. We figured that just getting the decoys out would be quite a challenge. But on the 9th with the aid of a pit heater we gave it an all-day near zero try and the migrating geese would have nothing to do with us.

We got skunked and Frank and Jeff were so steady about this acting like even this was a success, that it was another day before I realized how rotten I felt about this hunt. Because they were coming back on the 15th and 16th. I was greatly relieved when scouting on the evening of Thursday the 14th, I found geese in every field around our west pasture. We had an old pit there that had not been used in years. Even though the possibilities were high, I did not know how the old pit and the grass would look to the Heidelbaurs.

I should not have worried as Frank immediately assessed the selection of the site and pit as "perfect" and proceeded to prove it by two straight days of limit shooting over Jeff's bigfoot and silhouette decoys. We all enjoyed this very much and had me looking forward to 1996.

The second day after we had finished shooting our geese, as Jeff let on foot to go get their Suburban, Frankie (he wanted to be called that) and I were out in the decoys (we had taken pictures of us, the geese we shot and the decoys before Jeff left.) We were about to take down and pile the decoys when a thick fog rolled in and it was getting thicker and we could hear, but not see, lots of geese moving and soon, just by the noise, we could tell some were coming right at us.

Frankie said. "let's lay down." We did and out of the fog came lot of low flying geese. Flying just high enough to clear the fence where the pit was, and the flock flew right over us. We laid on our backs amongst the decoys, the geese never swerved or change they flight path, they just swept right over us and kept going. What a sight we had just witnessed.

I believe Frankie was 76 years old or so when I met him. His activeness, shooting and eagerness to get out and hunt woke me up and inspired me to get back in the game. He was an active leader in Ducks Unlimited and through his influence we donated goose hunts to them for their fundraising auctions. It turned out the hunters who bought the hunts were some wonderful hunters too. For some reason the doors of more good hunts were wide open when they came. With geese decoying and limits of geese shot.

I got to see Frank's call making place in the basement of his house. There were several steps to his call making and it was finished by a lady who could neatly write. She would put the new owner's name and the year it was made on it.

When Frank was over in the war on an island he flew out of, one morning he saw an exotic colorful pheasant like bird on the runway. He leaned out of the plane, took his rifle, and shot it. When we were down in his workshop, he showed me the feathers (they were 50 years old.) He used bit of them on the fishing lurers he made.

Frank and I traded letters back and forth. I had written a goose hunting history of hunting from start to finish. Kind of a chronicle of the history of hunting geese in our area from the time I started until then. He read it and said it was historical and encouraged me to write more.

We talked about faith in Christ. He said during his service in the war he got well acquainted with the Lord, constantly depending on Him for success in combat.

I was surprised to learn that Frank had been fighting diabetes for decades. He had air dime exercise bike that he rode daily. He said he did that so he would hunt, fish, and enjoy life.

He passed away a few years after I knew him, he had moved into a nice retirement home. His grandson, Todd, (who took over the duck and goose call business) said his friends would ask, "Why do you go and see that old man so much?"

He answered, "Because it is one of a few places I can go where I know and feel loved."

Frank's face would light up and he would say, "Toddy how are you?"

Rolly flew me down to Frank's funeral and it was full of hunters wearing his duck calls around their neck!

Jeff Heidelbauer (Frank's son) and Laurence Byrum at the divide fence south of the hunt camp. Photo taken by Frank Heidelbauer. December 15, 1995.

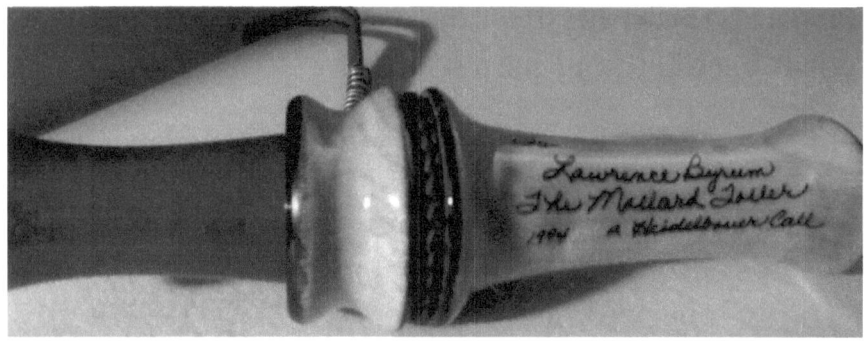

The Mallard Toller given to me by Frankie in 1994. outstanding workmanship.

Frank Heidelbauer at the home place. The first year he hunted with us. December 9, 1993.

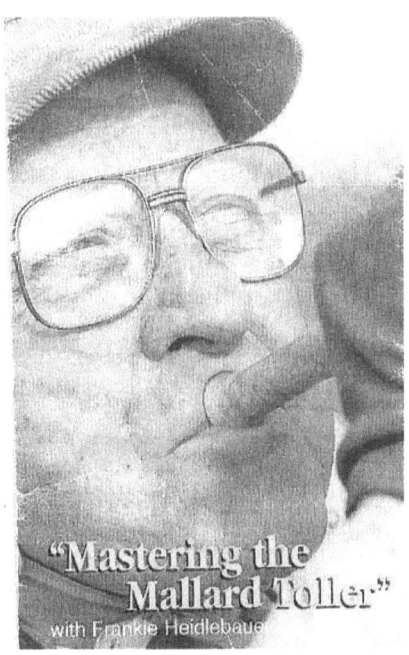

Frank Heidelbauer with one of the duck calls he made.

18 Cale Neal
lover of dogs and kids

By popular demand Cale is profiled here. In my book The Goose Hunters I focused so much on Karen and I's family, my parents and cousin Elliott Byrum (my close goose hunting friend) and things pertaining to that, of course it was limited. Cale's daughter Susan asked if her dad was in that. book and I said, "No maybe in the next book.".

Some years back I wrote the next book, and he is in there, but that book has not been published yet.

Yesterday, Greg asked me if Cale was in Goose Hunters I Have Known and I said, "no.' and Greg said, "Oh he should be!" and Karen thought so too.

I will tell this story like Larry Wilcox accused his mother, Gladys; of doing. Start in the middle and then work both ways. So, using part of the unpublished book, here goes.

How Hutch (short name for small Canada goose called Hutcheson) Got His Name. We have a killer in our family. We call him Hutch; in respectable circles he is known as Cale my sister Alice's husband. He is focused on one thing when hunting and that is shooting (he likes dogs, so we know his heart is good.)

One year (1975 I believe) after I had done all the sweating out the whole ball of wax to get ready for hunters Cale came (that is enough to send chills down the spine of all geese) along with member of the hunt club and a couple friends (Cale had been instrumental in suppling names for members in the club) and that morning they sat up in the milo field. With me driving and Greg and one of the Hugart boys in a field nearby right after sun-up, Greg and his partner got three geese out of a small flock of big geese and things were looking good.

The goose flock feeding at home included about 1500 lesser Canadas and about 500 big Canadas. We were hoping to get a few and get out before many were flying. The little fellers started coming and they were all headed for Cale swinging around and around the decoys either they were not close enough or Cale was waiting for big geese (I never knew) and the more they circled the bigger the flock got and after a bit it looked like about half the lessers were circling them and I was thinking it is going to be a long morning of sitting and waiting because nobody would shoot into a flock that size.

When they flared back and geese were dropping, I jammed the old pick-up in gear and went flying across the field picking up hunters and it seemed every goose on the river by then was there to witness the circus. When we got to the yard, I just went to doing chores and I milked the cow behind the barn and a few of the big geese started coming back from the east where they had taken temporary refuge from the fracas. Now they were gradually returning to the milo, having it-all to themselves because none of the smaller geese (which the hunters from the eastern part of the state called "hutches':) returned.

Cale came quietly around the-corner of the barn and said, "It looks like the big ones are getting back in there."

And Greg named him "Hutch" in honor of the way he had sorted the small geese from the big geese.

Alice and Cale did a lot of moving around. He was in the Navy, so they were in Florida and then they were in Aberdeen as Cale went to school at Northern. Then in Pierre he taught school (I think about 1958 a great goose year and Cale probably hunted some then with Elliott and I.)

Then they lived out at Igloo where the ammunition dumps are, they lived at Hot Springs, South Dakota, Fairmount, Minnesota, and then somewhere in St. Paul or Minneapolis where he got more schooling as he was following a path of being the top guy at hospitals, which he finally did in Watertown, South Dakota

While in Watertown he got to know Jim Adam and all the Adams. He and Alice were probably there long enough for daughters Virginia and Dawn and son Jeff to graduate from high school there.

Watertown is known for being the home of many hunters and the Adams family were right in the thick of that and likewise Cale. From Watertown he was able to make it out hunting with us part of the time.

From the time I first knew him, from 1954 and on, he loved to hunt. He was taken with the abundance of Mallard ducks back then, that used our area, and he would hunt them and walk a fencerow or two. Occasionally he would shoot a rooster, as all the hunters it seemed from eastern South Dakota were old hands at pheasant hunting.

Cale had grown up at Cark just a short distance from Watertown. So, he had his pheasant hunting style well developed. The big Canada geese were the birds we all put by themselves, and the goose hunters were spawning all over the place as the big birds went from small numbers to thousands along the Missouri River in the Oahe Lake complex. The fun started you might say, and Cale was in the right spot for several years even after he left Watertown he kept coming back and his daughters and Jeff and then sons-in-law had many good times whacking off geese at and around the old farmstead.

One of the best and bittersweet times I had with Cale was when Alice was in the hospital struggling to win her battle with sickness. She laughed at Cale and I's attempt to understand what she wanted us to do one day. They were living down in Grand Island Nebraska at the time and for the couple of days I was there it was just Cale and I staying at the house.

One snowy afternoon as we sat and visited in the living room, Cale told me this story (amongst many). When he was kid living around Clark, he had a special hunting buddy named Red. Red like Cale lived on a farm. Always hunting if they could they grabbed their shotguns and went out. One afternoon they trudged through the snow to Red's place, up into some hills and dells and on the way back they shot a pheasant, but it was a hen (not legal) and as they were nearing the farmstead they thought; better not bring a hen into the yard right then, maybe later so they tucked the hen under a snowbank. When they entered the edge of the yard the local game warden was there and came walking over and started talking to the boys. Red had a big old farm dog that was bouncing around and while Cale and Red visited with the warden the old dog went up the hill, dug the hen out and proudly came back with the pheasant in his mouth.

One of the hair-raising things at that time was traveling with Cale around Grand Island as he was starting to lose some of his abilities, and he might run a stop sign and not even blink.

After Alice died it was not long before Susan and her wonderful husband brought Cale up to her home in Worthing, South Dakota. Gary built an addition on to their home just for him. Cale's memory gradually left but he was always in contact with his family they all were wonderful to their dad and granddad.

That is where that old goose hunter's life ended, being loved daily. Is that not something? Susan gives her dad credit for leading her to believe in the Lord Jesus Christ.

Cale was a dog person it seemed if he got a dog, it did not matter whether it was a good useful dog or not. Once he had them, they stayed, and Alice was about the same.

He had a Springer Spaniel named Jessie. She was a good one. A natural upland game dog. Cale and her and I hunted together. I watched her work and as far as I know Cale never trained her, but she was so close to him (my interpretation) she just hunted close to him and listened to him, and Cale listened to her. She had some puppies. When other people got those puppies, Cale, followed up and checked to see if they were with people who took care of them.

He called me and asked if I wanted this one offspring of Jessie, it was a grown dog and it was not having a good life. Knowing Jessie and my need for a pheasant dog, I said yes. Karen and I met Cale at truck stop on the interstate and he gave us Scoobie. You have heard of her if you read much of my hunting stuff about a black and white purebred springer full of energy.

Karen and I disagreed to this day (4-4-20) how old Scoobie was then.

We will just say two and she gave me several years of help taking people pheasant hunting. She hunted ducks and grouse and even retrieved a goose. She was all go, and she taught my wonderful dog Hunter that he better retrieve, or she would, and he turned into the best dog I ever had. Cale had saved her from a life of not getting to do what she loved, hunt, hunt, hunt. And I learned a lot from her. I became a lot better dog person after the years with her.

Good job Cale.

Somehow Susan got my brother Ollie, my brother- in-law Neil Hanson and I to all come at same time to spend a little time with Cale in those last days he lived with her. Timing was crucial Cale was still able to let that personality of his come through and one morning the four of us drove over to Canton to have breakfast and Cale was our guide. He somehow faked his way to the right eating joint. That worked well. Then Cale was bent on going to the bank and to a certain store to buy what else? Dog food. I sat in the back seat with Cale as Ollie drove with Neil beside him and Cale is giving directions and soon, we are headed out the other end of town.

Ollie says, "Cale looks like we are lost." "Well," Cale says, "you're the one driving!"

I don't know if we found the bank, but we found the dog food place and Cale loaded up a bag about as big as you can get and headed back home.

There, we discovered the dog he was taken care of had a good stockpile already! It was a good trip even though Cale was slipping he still was able to laugh and trade barbs. Great timing Susan. I believe this was the best time to be able to visit Cale and do the things we did.

I am going to finish this with a goose hunt that shows pure enjoyment. As Cale and I hunted one afternoon. It was late in season on a cloudy day, chilly, but not bad. We were in a pit watching a few geese that kept moving around in the field north of us. Occasionally some would get up and fly off. I do not know why I was so sure, but I told Cale I think if we wait one of those small flocks will cut right through here and they did.

Cale had me shooting his double barrel and the little flock came right at us and I raised Cale's double up, rolled the lead goose right out and the geese broke climbing right around us on Cale's side, he shoots one as they go by. We pick the goose up. We had drove the 4010 down there, so we go back with Cale standing on the platform of the tractor and me driving. Cale was so tickled with that hunt (we both were) our waiting them out and getting those two geese.

As we drove, he was asking about the old 4010, John Deere tractor and we were happily visiting away! We went right on by the rock pile on the trail back to the old farmhouse (Lyle could have been watching) and that is a good way to end the story about Cale Neal goose hunter I knew.

Scoobie the Springer Spaniel, what a worker he was!

Cale Neal

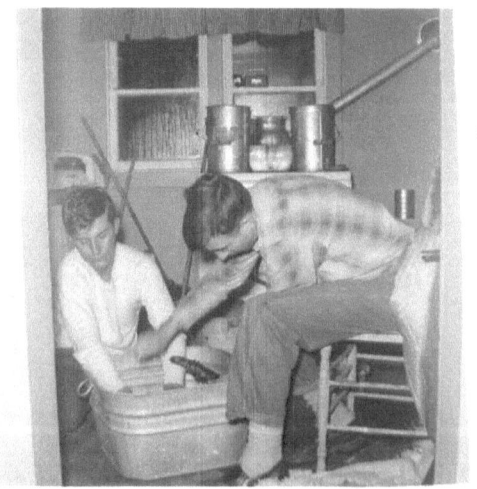

Laurence and Cale picking a goose I shot
while hunting with Doc Von Wald

Tim and Matt Thomas teamed up with Cale Neal and Scoobie to do some hunting. Probably a short poke around the camp shooting grouses and pheasants. I know they had much respect for each. The windmill in the background shows the place was over west, probably the first year we moved our original camp there 1997 or later.

19 Goosed In
Barb's bit

While helping Lawrence with the editing of "Goose Hunters I Have Known" I was looking for a story like the one I had heard from an extended family member. It's seemed my sister-in-law's husband Skip and some of his friends came from Wyoming to hunt geese with Lyle Sutton (my other sister-in-law's husband.) When they were out hunting and lying-in wait, the geese started to come in and lite. They came in, wave after wave and Lyle wouldn't let the men shoot. Afterward when they asked Lyle why he wouldn't let them shoot, he told them they were "goosed in" and if they had shot it would have scared all the geese away and that would be end of the hunt that day and days to come.

Needless to say, that is what they talked about the most on the way back to Wyoming. "We got goosed in!" "Dang, we were goosed in!" "That was the first time I've ever been goosed in!" etc. To this day there are still mentions of that day and being "goosed in."

In Laurence's stories he never referred to any instances of being goosed in, but he talked about "white outs" and "bonanzas" which are the same thing.

In his descriptions it sounds like it's a sight to behold, and I would love to see one, but being raised mostly in Southern California I am not about to go out and lay in the snow on a freezing day to view it.

I did however manage to snap a picture of Capitol Lake in Pierre, South Dakota when it was "goose-in."

"Goosed In" Capitol Lake in Pierre, South Dakota January 13, 2017.

20 Comments / Compliment

1983: "Better goose hunting than Maryland" John Akers, Ormand Beach, Florida

1983: "First place I've ever been that I got exactly as advertised," Tim Bigakle, San Francisco, California

1984, 1985, 1986, 1987, 1991, 1993: Always had a good time." Charley Caddell, Durango, Colorado.

1986, 1987: "Unique thing when the geese lit all around us and the noise they made." It was fun, we should get back again." Jeff Crisp. La Grange, Illinois.

1988, 1990, 1993: "Always had a good time." Ken Black, Warren, Pennsylvania.

1991: "Fantastic!" "More fun ever had on any hunting trip...it was the mix of game." Dr. Howard Carlson, Bloomfield Hills Ml.

1992: "Best hunt, best trip I've ever been on!" Bobby Shaefer, New Jersey

1993: "You have the best organized camp I've ever been too, and I have been to a lot of camps." James Novitsky, Grand Rapids, Michigan.

1993: "Best hunt... best grouse hunt I've been on in 20 years. Everything was good." John Fisher, Orient, Ohio.

1993: "I've never seen more pheasant... a memorable hunt...had a great time." Paul Remsen, Jacksonville, Florida.

1993: "Truly a great hunt, one I'll long remember and talk about." Frank Heidelbauer, Sioux Falls, South Dakota.

1994: "Best hunting day I've ever had in my life You can have anybody call me and I'll tell them same thing!" Dave Chenoweth, Illinois.

1995: "You most have the best pheasant fields in South Dakota." Chuck Pedrotte, Michigan

1996: "Leaving my gear, be here next year!" Matt Thomas, Jacksonville, Florida

1997: "Had a good time again." Howard Carlson, Michigan.

1997: "The goose hunting was so good, nothing more needs to be said." Paul Gilihan, Bloomfield Hills, Michigan

1998: "Tim and I just like to poke around and shot pheasants and we are leaving our gear for next year." Matt Thomas

www.ingramcontent.com/pod-product-compliance
Lightning Source LLC
Chambersburg PA
CBHW030153100526
44592CB00009B/256